# GROWING UP
## AT
# WAR
## MAUREEN·HILL

First published in the UK in Armada in 1989
Armada is an imprint of the Children's Division, part of the Collins Publishing Group, 8 Grafton Street, London WIX 3LA
Copyright © Maureen Hill 1989

# The Beginning of the War

Chamberlain, the British Prime Minister with Hitler and Mussolini

IMPERIAL WAR MUSEUM

## WAR IS DECLARED

On Sunday 3rd September 1939 Britain and France declared war on Germany. Many people had been expecting war for quite a long time although most people hoped it would never really happen.

When Germany invaded Poland on 1st September 1939 war became inevitable. Britain had promised to help Poland if such a thing happened. So on that Sunday at 11.15 a.m. nearly everyone in the country sat down to hear the Prime Minister, Neville Chamberlain, say on the radio:

"This morning the British Ambassador in Berlin handed the German government a final Note stating that unless we heard from them by eleven o'clock that they were prepared at once to withdraw their troops from Poland a state of war would exist between us.

"I have to tell you now that no such undertaking has been received, and that consequently this country is at war with Germany."

From 1933 onwards Germany, under Hitler, had been building up its armies and its supplies of weapons, tanks, aeroplanes and ships.

Once Hitler had power in Germany he began to take over in countries like Austria

## HITLER'S RISE TO POWER

Adolf Hitler was ruling Germany when war broke out. He had become leader of the Nazi Party and Chancellor (like Prime Minister) in 1933. Germany was then in a very weak position because:

● Germany had lost the First World War (1914-18).

● Britain, France and the U.S.A. made Germany pay so much money as compensation for starting World War I that the German government had no money.

● Inflation was so high that German banks printed bank notes worth 100 billion marks — and even that amount of money would only buy a few things to eat.

● Many people had no work and those who earned wages found their money nearly worthless.

The German people were so desperate that they turned to the first person whom they believed would make Germany a better place to live — and that person was Adolf Hitler, leader of the Nazi Party.

| 30th September 1938 | 15th March 1939 | 31st March 1939 |
|---|---|---|
| Prime Minister Neville Chamberlain comes home to Britain after meeting and talking with Hitler in Germany. He says he believes that there will be "peace for our time" and war will be avoided. | Hitler's Germany takes over in Czechoslovakia. | Britain and France promise to help Poland if she is attacked by Germany. |

and Czechoslovakia. He ruled these countries and Germany with the help of the army and a secret police force. He began a campaign of hatred against Jewish people and anyone else he did not approve of.

## THE PACT OF STEEL

Though many countries disapproved of Germany, there was one country which pledged its support for what Hitler was doing and that was Italy. In May 1939 Germany signed an agreement with the Italian government and this was called the Pact of Steel. The Italian government was very similar to the Nazi government in Germany. In both countries the army and police kept strict control of the people under very severe laws passed by the government.

## GERMANY TAKES OVER EUROPE

Britain and France both had a lot of power and influence in the world and became worried that a country like Germany would become more powerful than them. They watched as Germany took over Austria and Czechoslovakia and Italy took over Abyssinia (now called Ethiopia) in Africa but they refused to accept the German invasion of Poland.

For the first year of the war, Britain and France were not strong enough to stop Hitler and Germany. By May

## MAP OF EUROPE ON THE DAY WAR BEGAN

### KEY

 Area of Germany when Hitler came to power (1933)

Area ruled by Germany at the beginning of World War II (3rd Sept 1939)

L = LUXEMBOURG
NL = NETHERLANDS
⬤ ⬤ = SIEGFRIED LINE

| 23rd August 1939 | 1st September 1939 | 3rd September 1939 |
|---|---|---|
| Germany and Russia sign an agreement not to go to war with each other. This makes Hitler think nothing can stop him invading Poland. | Hitler's Germany invades Poland. | Britain and France declare war on Germany. |

1940 Germany had taken over Norway, Denmark, Holland, Belgium and Luxembourg and was beginning to take over France. The British Prime Minister, Neville Chamberlain, resigned because of this failure, and on 10th May 1940 Winston Churchill took over as Prime Minister and became famous as Britain's wartime leader.

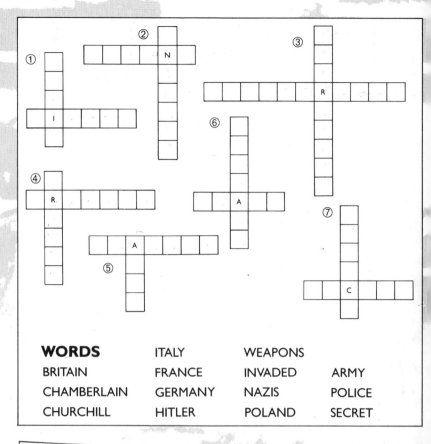

**WORDS**

| | | | |
|---|---|---|---|
| | ITALY | WEAPONS | |
| BRITAIN | FRANCE | INVADED | ARMY |
| CHAMBERLAIN | GERMANY | NAZIS | POLICE |
| CHURCHILL | HITLER | POLAND | SECRET |

## THINGS TO DO

**1** Your Operations Map: Make a large copy of the map on Page 3. Colour each country a different colour. Put your map up on the wall. Using paper and pins make some small flags showing Nazi Germany's flag. Stick flags in Austria, Czechoslovakia and Poland to show they have been taken over by Germany. Keep this map and you can add information to it as you read through the book. It will be like an army's operations map.

glue

pin →

**2** Above are seven crossword pairs. Each member of the pair has some connection to the other, apart from the letter in common. From the given list of words match the pairs and fit them into a suitable grid.

**3** During the war there were many cartoon drawings of Churchill and Hitler. Try drawing your own cartoon for each of these men.

| 1st-4th September 1939 | 5th September 1939 | 11th September 1939 |
|---|---|---|
| Evacuation of people from the cities begins in Britain. | American President Roosevelt says the U.S.A. will not become involved in the war. Neither Britain and France nor Germany will be allowed to buy weapons from the U.S.A. The U.S.A. will try to encourage talks to stop the war. | The first soldiers of the British Expeditionary Force (B.E.F.) land in France to march to fight the German army. |

# EVACUATION

Britain had not prepared for war by building tanks and aeroplanes, ships and other weapons but it had made plans to evacuate, that is move people, if war should start. It was believed that if war did begin, Germany would immediately send aeroplanes to bomb British cities, putting civilians at risk. So the very day that Hitler invaded Poland, evacuation began in Britain.

Some people made their own arrangements for evacuation, sometimes sending women and children as far away as Australia, Canada and the U.S.A. The government also arranged for large numbers of schoolchildren, mothers and children under school age, pregnant women and handicapped people to be evacuated.

## EVACUATION AREAS

Britain was divided into three types of area:
1. *Evacuation areas* which were places in danger of being bombed.
2. *Reception areas* in country towns and villages where people were expected to offer rooms (billets) in their homes to people from evacuation areas.
3. *Neutral areas* where no one was to either leave or send evacuees.

In the first week of the war nearly four million people moved from evacuation to reception areas.

## THE JOURNEY

Children to be evacuated without their parents were sent to their school with a luggage label showing their name and address attached to their coats. They carried only a few clothes, a packed lunch, and a gas mask. Teachers and helpers took the children on buses and trains to the reception areas.

Sometimes the journey was quite short but for some the trip lasted over twelve hours. Most children arrived exhausted in places they had never even heard of.

## TOWN MEETS COUNTRY

Many stories are told of the shock that both city and country people had when they met during evacuation. In 1939 poor people had much less than they have now. Many children

Empire lasts for a thousand years, men will still say: THIS WAS THEIR FINEST HOUR
—The Premier, last night

**Let All The Children Go To Safety**

THE six-day evacuation from London has ended. These boys and girls have been sent by their parents to the West Country. But about 340,000 children remain in Greater London.

**You Must Carry Your Gas Mask**

THE six-day evacuation from London has ended. These boys and girls have been sent by their parents to the West Country. But about 340,000 children remain in Greater London.

Arrangements should be made at once to remove all children from crowded cities—if necessary to Canada, which has offered to shelter thousands.

France's Foreign Minister has said that his country " has merely asked Germany under what conditions she would consent to stop the slaughter of French children." We shall fight all the better if we know that the children are safe.

from poor city areas had no water in their homes so they hardly ever washed themselves or their clothes.

Many country people were horrified and saddened to find how dirty and full of minor infections — like scabies and

| 30th September 1939 | 16th October 1939 | 4th November 1939 |
| --- | --- | --- |
| Poland is defeated and divided between Germany and Russia who invaded from the east on 17th September. | A German U-boat (submarine) sinks a British battleship, the *Royal Oak*, in Scapa Flow, the ship's home base, off the north coast of Scotland. | The U.S.A., although it still will not become involved in the fighting, agrees to sell weapons to Britain and France. |

impetigo — some of the city children were. Sometimes the surprise was the other way round and children from homes with baths and electric lights found themselves staying in farm-labourers' cottages with no running water or electricity.

For many children it was the first time they had ever seen the countryside and they were amazed by real animals that they

had only ever seen before in pictures.

On 29th October 1939 an essay by a ten-year-old from London was read out on BBC radio's nine o'clock news:

"The cow is a mamal. It has six sides, right, left and upper and below. At the back it has a tail, on which hangs a brush. The head is for the purpose of growing horns and so the mouth can be somewhere. The horns are to butt with and the mouth is to moo with. Under the cow hangs the milk. When people milk, the milk comes and there is never an end to the supply. The cow has a fine sense of smell, one can smell it far away. This is the reason for the fresh air in the country."

## ADOPTED HOMES

Some children found the countryside disturbing and were desperate to return home, while others enjoyed the freedom to be able to play in the fields and lanes. Many children grew to love both the countryside and the families who took them in, so that when parents came to take them home some children did not want to go. One boy, evacuated from Edinburgh to the surrounding countryside could only be persuaded to leave his adopted home and family by his mother telling him he was only going home for a holiday.

Some evacuees stayed with their adopted families for the whole of the war. However, the first year of the war saw less bombing raids than expected and many evacuees returned home. Despite efforts by the government's Ministry of Information to stop the return, by the time the blitz really started in August 1940 most children were back with their mothers. Many decided they could not bear to be parted from their children again and risked keeping them at home.

However, some children were evacuated for a second time and in many cases did not return until the end of the war.

### OTHER EVACUEES

- The treasures of the National Gallery were evacuated and stored in a disused slate quarry in North Wales.
- The village of Overton in Hampshire became the home of the Bank of England.
- The BBC set up its main centre in a country house near Evesham in Worcestershire.

## THINGS TO DO

**1** Imagine you are an evacuee — write a letter home to your parents telling them about your journey and where you are staying.

**2** If you had to be evacuated today — where would you go? Plan how you would get there.

**3** Design an advertisement to go in a women's magazine to encourage mothers to evacuate their children to the country.

| 8th November 1939 |
|---|
| An attempt is made on Hitler's life when a bomb explodes under the platform from which he has just made a speech. Hitler escapes unhurt. |

| 30th November 1939 |
|---|
| Russia, under the leadership of Stalin, invades Finland. |

| 17th December 1939 |
|---|
| The *Graf Spee* – a German battleship is sunk by her captain and crew on orders from Hitler, so that the British Navy cannot take her. |

# school

The War started at the very end of the school holidays. To the delight of schoolchildren throughout the country the government announced that the summer holiday would continue indefinitely. However, in the countryside the joy was short-lived. Most country schools were re-opened by the middle of September, even if it meant only part-time school. There were so many local children and evacuees to use the school buildings that often they had to take it in turn to go to school.

## PART - TIME SCHOOLING

In the towns and cities it took much longer to get children back to school. Schools could only teach the number of pupils they had air raid shelter space for. This meant that until enough shelters were built, children often had to take it in turns to go to school, just like children in the country.

Sometimes lessons were in churches or rooms lent by parents but even this was only part-time, often no more than two hours a day.

With so many children out of school for long periods - many with no parents at home because father was away fighting and mother was working in a weapons' factory - there was a huge increase in vandalism and hooliganism. Public air raid shelters were wrecked so many times by children that in the end they had to be kept locked. The government was therefore forced to try to make sure that schools ran as normally as possible.

## POOR QUALITY EDUCATION

Even when things settled down, there were often reasons for children receiving little or no education at all:

- Some schools were taken over for other uses such as rest centres for bombed-out families.
- In other cases the schools themselves were destroyed in bombing raids.
- Many teachers were called up to fight in the army and the few teachers left were moved around the country to wherever it was considered they were most needed.

When a teacher and suitable buildings could be found there were difficulties in getting enough books and writing materials:

- Paper was very scarce and in an exercise book a pupil had to use every inch of

| 8th January 1940 | 26th January 1940 | 13th March 1940 |
| --- | --- | --- |
| Food rationing begins with each person allowed 4 oz bacon; 4 oz butter and 12 oz sugar per week. As yet no other food is rationed. | Women who have taken jobs in factories doing work that was only done by men before demand to be paid the same wages as men. | The war between Russia and Finland ends. Large areas of Finland are taken over by the Russians. There is great praise for tiny Finland which fought hard. |

7

space; front and back covers, no margin, top and bottom lines.

- Pupils had to write either with very thin and breakable pencils which had to be used down to the last 2 cms or with scratchy nibs in holders which were dipped into an ink well.
- Books to read and learn from were also difficult to find and so few new books were printed that if a book was ripped or became tatty it could not be replaced.

All these problems meant that children's education suffered and it was possible to find schools where in a class of seven-year-olds not one could read. By the end of the war there were far more children considered backward in reading and writing than there had been before the war. However, if children

missed out on reading, writing and arithmetic − the three main subjects − they learnt a good deal about other things during the war. The evacuees learned about the countryside and they in turn taught the country children about their way of life. Teachers were forced to spend a large amount of time teaching things like cooking, gardening, keeping animals for food, knitting and sewing so that children too could help with the "war effort".

**At the sound of the Siren . . . .**
a suit to keep the children warm and cosy in an emergency

**TOFFEE of the BETTER KIND**

## A NEW EDUCATION SYSTEM

One thing the war did was to show the unfairness of the education system in England and Wales. For most children a secondary school education was not possible. They attended an elementary school from five to fourteen and had no special subject education. In 1944 the Minister for Education, R.A. Butler, designed a new school system for England and Wales:

- After the war, all children, from the age of eleven, would be given a secondary education in one of three types of school: grammar, technical or secondary modern.
- The school leaving age was raised to fifteen and would be increased to sixteen as soon as possible.

LIVES OF FAMOUS PIRATES
THE NOTORIOUS
**BLACKBEARD**

The **FLYING BOMB**
BRITISH MADE

| 9th April 1940 | 15th April 1940 | 10th May 1940 |
|---|---|---|
| Germany invades Norway and Denmark. | British and French troops land in Norway to fight the Germans but by 2nd May they have begun to retreat. | Germany invades Holland, Belgium and Luxembourg. Chamberlain resigns as Prime Minister of Britain. |

## 3 CROSSWORD CLUES:

### ACROSS

1. Another word for learning (9)
7. The initials of the man responsible for designing a new school system (2)
8. The teacher might tell a pupil to ---- a line under the title (4)
9. The reason for schools being disrupted (3)
11. A school subject (3)
12. During the war a pupil would have measured 2.54cms as one ---- (4)
15. This is what some children had to do to avoid being hurt in air raids at home (8)
17. The Royal Air Force, in short (3)
19. Many children had to spend the war separated from the ---- they knew and loved (6)
20. This writing instrument had to be used to the last 2cms (6)
21. Many children were late in learning to do this, because they missed so much school during the war (4)

### DOWN

2. Something you might do in an art lesson (7)
3. When school buildings could not be found, lessons might take place in a hall belonging to one of these (8)
4. One of the sections the school year is broken up into (4)
5. These birds are symbols of wisdom and learning (4)
6. Part of an ink pen (3)
10. One of the things a pupil does with a pen (6)
13. During a ---- pupils would have to take cover in the school's shelter (4)
14. War-time Minister for Education (6)
16. For children evacuated to the country it would be easy to go on a school ---- to visit a local farm (4)
18. Despite many difficulties school could still be ----, during the war (3)

## THINGS TO DO

**1** Imagine you arrive at school one morning to find it has been destroyed by a bomb in the night. Write about what you would miss about school and how you would use your time if you were off school for long.

**2** Using bits and pieces of junk materials make a collage picture of a bombed-out school.

| 13th May 1940 | 14th May 1940 | 20th May 1940 |
|---|---|---|
| Churchill, now Prime Minister of a coalition government makes a speech in which he says, "I have nothing to offer but blood, toil, tears and sweat." | An appeal is broadcast on the radio for men to join the Local Defence Volunteers (later to become known as the Home Guard and jokingly called "Dad's Army"). | Germany's attack on Holland, Belgium and Luxembourg has succeeded and Hitler's Army moves on into France. |

# DUNKIRK

## BLITZKRIEG

After Germany had invaded and defeated Poland in September 1939, Hitler turned his attention to Norway and Denmark. Here he used the same method of *blitzkrieg* (meaning "lightning war" in German) to defeat them. This involved concentrating large amounts of army and air power in one mighty force and pushing through a country's defences. The army would then drive deep behind the front line and cut the country's lines of communication and supply.

Next, he invaded Holland, Belgium and Luxembourg and when they had surrendered, the German troops, together with their tanks and airforce, carried the fighting on into France.

## DUNKIRK

Throughout the "lightning war" the German Army seemed unstoppable and the British and French armies were constantly pushed back. Eventually they reached Dunkirk and the beaches of the English Channel, and could go no further.

Everything seemed lost until — for some still unknown

reason — the German tanks and soldiers stopped moving forward for 48 hours. Perhaps Hitler thought that Britain would surrender when she saw that France was defeated and realized how hopeless the situation was. Whatever the reason, the pause in the Germans' advance gave Britain the chance to bring home 338,226 British and French

soldiers between 26th May and 3rd June 1940.

## CROSSING THE CHANNEL

The only way the troops could be brought back from Dunkirk was by boat. Soldiers, under fire from German planes, had to wade out into the sea from the beaches to the waiting boats. And what a selection of boats there was! The Navy, of course, had its ships there, but many men were returned home by less conventional boats. The channel ferries were also there, as were thousands of small

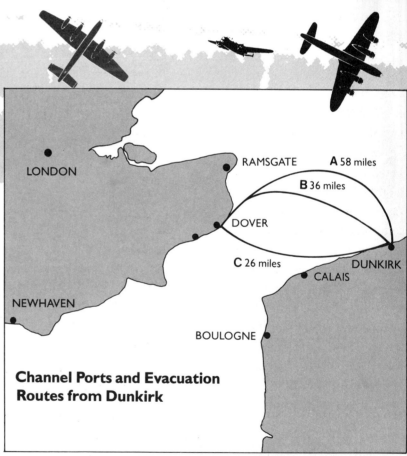

**Channel Ports and Evacuation Routes from Dunkirk**

| 26th May-3rd June 1940 | 5th June 1940 | 10th June 1940 |
|---|---|---|
| Britain manages to rescue 338,226 British and French troops from Dunkirk. | Germany launches an all out attack on France. | Italy, Germany's ally, declares war on Britain and France. |

# 338,226 MEN EVACUATED

boats whose owners had responded to radio appeals for help. Fishing boats and pleasure boats of all shapes and sizes set sail for Dunkirk.

The journey across the English Channel was very dangerous. There were wrecks and mines to avoid and constant attacks by the German Luftwaffe. Nevertheless, many ships made the trip more than once.

## HOME

Once home the troops had to be fed and the wounded tended. Organizations like the *Women's Voluntary Service* (which later became the Women's Royal Voluntary Service or WRVS) arranged cooking and washing facilities for the tired, dirty and starving troops. *ENSA* (Entertainments National Service Association) arranged films and shows for the soldiers who often had to wait several hours and even days before they could be transported from the coast to their army bases.

## A VICTORY FROM DEFEAT

To people in Britain, the evacuation of the troops from Dunkirk seemed like a miracle. Newspaper reports and radio broadcasts made what was really a defeat sound like a victory. Indeed in many ways it was a victory for had Britain not been able to rescue all those soldiers there would not have been enough men left to continue the fighting against Germany. Britain would have had to surrender.

# DUNKIRK —LAST MEN GO

## THINGS TO DO

**1** Experiment with cartons and lids to make different types of boats.

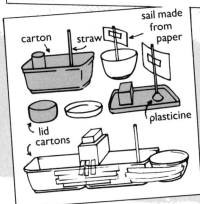

carton · straw · sail made from paper · plasticine · lid cartons

When you have made your boats, float them in some water and experiment loading them with stones. See how many stones each type of boat can take and still keep afloat and be blown across the water.

**2** Write two newspaper stories about the evacuation of the troops from Dunkirk. One story is for a British newspaper and the other for a German newspaper. Try to set the stories out exactly as they would appear in a newspaper.

**3** Mark Dunkirk and the English Channel ports on your operations map. Use your Nazi flags to show that Norway, Denmark, Holland, Belgium, and Luxembourg are all under German control (check the chronology to see what happened to France).

---

| 14th June 1940 | 22nd June 1940 | 25th June 1940 |
|---|---|---|
| German troops capture Paris and the Nazi flag flies from the Eiffel Tower. | France surrenders to Germany and Britain is left to fight alone. | German troops are issued with English phrase books in preparation for Germany's invasion of Britain. |

# AIR ATTACK

## BATTLE OF BRITAIN

After Dunkirk and France's surrender, Hitler's next move was to try to invade Britain. In a plan, codenamed *Operation Sea Lion*, Germany aimed to send over troop-ships to land in Britain on 15th September 1940. This date was chosen as having the most suitable tides for invasion by sea. For the plan to succeed it was necessary for the German airforce (the Luftwaffe) to destroy the RAF (the British Royal Airforce) so that soldiers could land without being attacked from the air.

In July and August 1940 the Luftwaffe and the RAF had their own battle. There were a great many *dogfights* over Southern England. A dogfight involved two planes trying to shoot one another out of the sky. Most of these fights took place during the day and many people witnessing them learned to identify the sight and sounds of both sides' planes.

As well as dogfights the Luftwaffe tried to bomb RAF airfields and aircraft factories in an attempt to destroy the

Bomb damage at Bank Station, London

MUSEUM OF LO[N]

planes and their landing areas and prevent any replacements being built.

The RAF was judged to have won this battle when by 15th September 1940 the Luftwaffe had lost 1733 planes to the RAF's 915.

Because of the bravery of the RAF and the hard work of the workers in the aircraft factories, Hitler was forced to

abandon Operation Sea Lion and the invasion of Britain never took place.

## THE BLITZ

Although an invasion was avoided, the civilians of Britain had begun to know what it was like to be under fire. August 1940 saw the first of the bombing raids that everyone had feared from the beginning of the war.

| 30th June 1940 | 1st July 1940 | 3rd July 1940 |
|---|---|---|
| Guernsey is the first of the Channel Islands to be occupied by German troops. | The government of France moves from Paris to Vichy. It has become a government like that of Nazi Germany under the leadership of Marshal Petain. Many French people disagree with his policies. | The British Navy destroys a large part of the French Navy at a base in North Africa. This is to prevent it being used by the Germans to sink British ships. |

On 7th September 1940 there was a huge attack on London which left much of the city in flames; flames which could be seen more than 30 miles away. This was the beginning of what became known as the *London Blitz*. "Blitz" was taken from the German word meaning lightning and, like lightning, the planes struck and left everything ablaze.

From 7th September to 2nd November that year London

was bombed every single night. After that the Luftwaffe began attacks on towns and cities like Southampton, Portsmouth, Bristol, Glasgow, Liverpool, Birmingham and Coventry.

In the bombing raids on Britain in 1940 and 1941, 43,000 civilians died. By June 1941 the German planes were needed to fight elsewhere and the raids almost stopped.

## BOMBING OF GERMANY

All the time the Luftwaffe were bombing Britain, the RAF were bombing Germany. The capital city of Berlin, the port of Hamburg and cities such as

| | |
|---|---|
| Marshal of the Royal Air Force | Flight-Lieutenant |
| Air Chief Marshal | Flying Officer |
| Air Marshal | Pilot Officer |
| Air Vice-Marshal | |
| Air Commodore | |
| Group-Captain | |
| Wing-Commander | |
| Squadron-Leader | |

HOME OFFICE

# THE PROTECTION OF YOUR HOME AGAINST AIR RAIDS

READ THIS BOOK THROUGH THEN KEEP IT CAREFULLY

## GERMAN FIGHTERS    Scale

MESSERSCHMIDT 109

MESSERSCHMIDT 110

HEINKEL 113

FOCKE-WULF 198

## GERMAN BOMBERS    Sca

---

**10th July 1940**
The Battle of Britain begins. This was Hitler's all out attack to try to invade and defeat Britain.

**31st July 1940**
The French government in Vichy says any French person who joins a foreign army will be sentenced to death. This is to try to stop French soldiers fighting with the British against the Germans.

**9th August 1940**
First bombing raid on Birmingham, centre for a great deal of weapon production.

Dresden and Cologne suffered just as much as places in Britain. It is interesting to note that the people who had suffered in the Blitz in England did not want the people of Germany to suffer in the same way. Opinion polls found that most people in London and other bombed areas did not want the RAF to bomb Germany, while those people living in areas which were never bombed approved of the bombing raids on Germany.

In 1942 and 1943, the RAF carried out some very heavy bombing raids on Germany. On 30th May 1942 the RAF sent 1000 bomber planes to drop more than 2000 tons of bombs on the city of Cologne in an attempt to stop the production of weapons there.

## V WEAPONS

The only other air attacks against Britain were the V1 and V2 rocket bombs launched from Europe in 1944. They became known as *buzz bombs* or *doodle bugs*. Having no pilot and being difficult to shoot down, they were sent over in the daytime and proved very frightening.

## BOMBING DOES NOT WORK!

The many bombing raids during the war were to try to do two things:
1. To stop the manufacture of weapons;
2. To frighten the civilians in the hope they would then force the government to surrender.

Neither of these plans ever succeeded. The bombing of Cologne destroyed two hundred factories but the production of weapons was only stopped for five days. It was the same story elsewhere. People worked harder to keep the weapons factories going and the bombing only seemed to make everyone more determined to survive and win.

## THINGS TO DO

**1** Find out if anywhere near you suffered bomb damage.

**2** Make silhouettes of World War II planes in card – you can copy them from this section or find other examples. Make a mobile with the plane silhouettes using a coat hanger and/or pieces of wood.

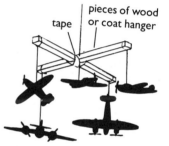

tape    pieces of wood or coat hanger

**3** Imagine you lived in London or another bombed city during the war. Write a letter to a friend evacuated to the country and tell them about your experience of the bombing.

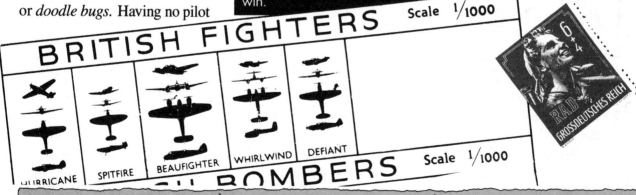

BRITISH FIGHTERS    Scale 1/1000

| HURRICANE | SPITFIRE | BEAUFIGHTER | WHIRLWIND | DEFIANT |

BOMBERS    Scale 1/1000

| 25th August 1940 | 26th August 1940 | 27th August 1940 |
| --- | --- | --- |
| The Luftwaffe carry out their first bombing raid on London. | The RAF drop bombs and propaganda leaflets on Berlin, Germany's capital city. | The Luftwaffe bomb 21 cities in Britain. |

# THE BLACKOUT

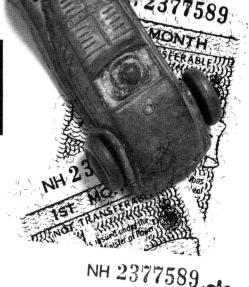

Even before the war, the government had made plans for *Air Raid Protection* (A.R.P.). They had assumed that most bombing raids would be carried out during the *daylight* hours, but in the event, the Germans risked only very few daytime raids. This was because both the RAF and the anti-aircraft gunners — including large numbers of women — were very successful in shooting down enemy planes.

## INSIDE THE HOME

From the beginning of the war, precautions were taken to "black out" all lights. This was essential as it became clear that most bombing raids would take place at night. The light from even one house could be used by an enemy plane as a target on which to drop its bombs. Very often planes would drop incendiary bombs which would start fires and light up target areas so that more planes could fly over and drop their bombs. This made the Fire Services' job very important during the war, although civilians were also shown how to put out fires.

Each night everyone had to make sure that not one chink of light escaped from the windows and doors of their home. Heavy curtains or blinds could be effective but some windows were simply painted over or covered with cardboard or thick paper for the whole of the war.

MUSEUM OF LONDON

NH 2377589

Motor Fuel Ration Book

MOTOR CAR
1501 – 2200
CC

14 – 19
H.P.

Registered No. of Vehicle

Date and Office of Issue

This book is the property of Her Majesty's Government

The coupons in this book authorise the furnishing and acquisition of the number of units of motor fuel specified on the coupons.

## OUTSIDE THE HOME

Going out of their home at night, people had to remember to switch off the light before opening an outside door. Once outside, there were no street lights and what few cars, buses and lorries there were, were fitted with special headlamps that gave out very little light.

Lampposts and kerb edges were painted with white or luminous paint but this did not prevent a number of deaths caused by people walking into

| 1st September 1940 | 7th September 1940 | 17th September 1940 |
| --- | --- | --- |
| The RAF's first attack on the German city of Munich. | The London Blitz begins. Massive numbers of bomber and fighter planes attack London, leaving the city in flames. | Hitler decides to postpone indefinitely "Operation Sea Lion" – the codename for the plan to invade Britain. The Battle of Britain is judged to be won. |

GROSSDEUTSCHES REICH

solid objects in the dark. Road accidents, too, increased despite the fact that petrol rationing meant there were very few vehicles on the road.

In opinion polls carried out in Britain the blackout was always top of most people's list of what they found most inconvenient about the war. Not only did people have to spend time everyday blacking out their own homes, or walking in the pitch black streets, but the blackout also made working conditions difficult for many people.

## AT WORK

Night work in the open air, on farms and places like railway sidings had to be done with no light. In many factories it was easier to simply paint and seal the windows or board them over to stop light escaping rather than keep altering curtains and blinds. However, this meant that even during the day the windows could not be opened. Workers had to operate in hot factories with no ventilation and only artificial lighting.

The blackout ended on 17th September 1944 to be replaced by the *dim out*. Although the war had not ended at that time it was felt it was going well enough for there to be no risk of any bombing raids.

There were laws against allowing light to escape from buildings and by the time the blackout ended, nearly one million people had been prosecuted for breaking the blackout regulations. Most people were fined but one man was sentenced in February 1940 to one month's hard labour for allowing light to be seen from his house.

| 27th September 1940 | 7th October 1940 | 10th October 1940 |
|---|---|---|
| Japan, Germany and Italy sign an agreement to help each other economically and in the fighting. They are known together as the AXIS POWERS. | Germany and Italy invade Rumania. | Part of St. Paul's Cathedral is destroyed in the bombing raids that hit London every night. |

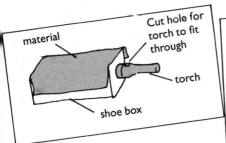

Labels on diagram: material, Cut hole for torch to fit through, torch, shoe box

## THINGS TO DO

**1** Using a torch and a box (a shoe box is ideal) experiment with different types and thicknesses of material to find out what blacks out the light in the most effective way.

**2** Try to black out a window in your home. Remember not a pin prick of light should be seen from outside.

## **3** WORDSEARCH
Can you find the following 24 words hidden horizontally, vertically or diagonally in the grid.

| | |
|---|---|
| Air raid | Gas Mask |
| Anti-aircraft | Incendiary |
| A.R.P. | Inconvenient |
| Blackout | Light |
| Blinds | Luminous |
| Bombing | Mickey Mouse |
| Box | Night |
| Chemical | Precautions |
| Curtains | Protection |
| Dark | Regulations |
| Dim out | Ventilation |
| Fires | Windows |

## GAS MASKS

In making plans for A.R.P. the government had expected the Germans to use chemical gas bombs just like those used against soldiers in the First World War.

Before the war started, therefore, everyone was issued with a gas mask in a box. Children had Mickey Mouse-style gas masks with red rubber faces. Everyone was required by law to carry their gas mask wherever they went.

There were many practices in the streets to make sure everyone knew how to put their gas mask on quickly. An A.R.P. warden would give the signal for a gas attack by sounding a football rattle in the street.

No real gas attack ever took place and so by the middle of 1940 most people had stopped carrying their gas masks.

Wordsearch grid:

| O | G | B | L | M | S | O | W | E | V | T | I | D | E | M | R |
|---|---|---|---|---|---|---|---|---|---|---|---|---|---|---|---|
| I | N | C | O | N | V | E | N | I | E | N | T | A | T | I | O |
| N | C | H | E | M | I | B | B | O | N | S | T | R | U | C | K |
| C | H | E | O | L | B | O | X | F | T | D | S | K | I | K | S |
| E | A | M | S | W | E | I | G | H | I | B | O | R | C | E | N |
| N | T | I | S | T | O | B | N | R | L | L | E | W | E | Y | T |
| D | I | C | N | A | W | L | S | G | A | I | J | P | S | M | P |
| I | M | A | I | R | R | A | I | D | T | G | L | V | E | O | P |
| A | T | L | G | P | L | C | A | T | I | H | O | B | N | U | R |
| R | W | I | H | N | B | K | L | F | O | T | I | L | R | S | E |
| Y | F | L | T | I | G | O | H | T | N | A | N | I | T | E | C |
| C | I | R | R | E | G | U | L | A | T | I | O | N | S | T | A |
| A | R | I | C | U | R | T | A | I | N | S | N | D | S | B | U |
| L | E | I | D | I | M | O | U | T | N | D | S | S | L | U | T |
| M | S | G | A | S | M | A | S | K | I | N | O | U | S | P | I |
| A | N | T | I | A | I | R | C | R | A | F | T | A | I | N | O |
| T | B | P | R | O | T | E | C | T | I | O | N | O | M | B | N |
| I | N | G | G | R | A | S | S | L | U | M | I | N | O | U | S |

---

| 28th October 1940 | 14th November 1940 | 22nd November 1940 |
|---|---|---|
| Italy invades Greece from Albania in the north. Italy had occupied Albania before the war began. | Coventry suffers the heaviest bombing raid of the war. The whole of its 500-year-old cathedral is destroyed. | The Greeks have beaten back the invading Italian troops. |

# SHELTERS

## ANDERSON SHELTERS

The Blackout did not stop bombing raids; it only made it more difficult for the bombers to find their targets. It was obvious that people would be at risk of death or injury from the bombing so some sort of shelter or protection had to be provided for everyone. For homes with gardens the

government supplied the materials for an *Anderson* shelter and it was the responsibility of the householders to build the shelter themselves. This simple shelter, made of corrugated iron, had to be installed three feet (91cm) deep in the garden and covered with at least eighteen inches (46cm) of earth. When finished, the

Anderson shelter was only about two metres by two metres or the size of the average garden shed.

## OTHER SHELTERS

People without an Anderson shelter would either have to shelter under the stairs, in a ground floor cupboard of their own home or use a public shelter. The government had constructed a variety of public shelters housing anything from fifty to more than a thousand people. Factories and schools also had to have their own air raid shelters.

People who lived in strongly built flats or tenements with no nearby shelters often had to take refuge in ground floor stair

wells or corridors. The outside walls of these buildings were often reinforced by sandbags or an extra wall and the door was protected from blast by a brick wall, built a bit like a porch.

## INSIDE THE SHELTERS

It had not been expected that people would have to spend whole nights in their shelter as it was thought most air raids would take place in daylight. Conditions in the shelters were often unpleasant. An Anderson shelter was usually lit only by a torch, candle or oil lamp. There was no toilet, no way of heating any food and the deafening sound of bombs dropping all around outside. The atmosphere was stuffy so it was difficult to get a good night's

People would often grow vegetables on top of the Anderson shelter in the 18 inches (46cm) of earth

steel rails to strengthen the shelter

corrugated iron

3 feet (91cm) deep

MUSEUM OF LONDON

## SIRENS

The newly developed *radar* made it possible to have some early warning of enemy planes approaching. Then the air raid siren, a long wailing noise, would be sounded and everyone would have to make for shelter. When the planes returned home another siren would sound the "All Clear" and people knew it was safe to leave their shelters.

During the London Blitz, when London was bombed all night, every night for two months, people did not wait for the sound of the sirens but went straight to their shelter from work, slept the night there and went to work from the shelter in the morning. If they stayed in a public shelter there would be little chance of having a wash or even much of a breakfast.

sleep in the Anderson shelter.

Sleep was just as difficult in public shelters. Although after a few weeks of the Blitz public shelters were provided with heat, light, toilets and sometimes canteens, it was still difficult to settle to rest. Hundreds or even thousands of people shared a shelter, some of whom spent the time playing games, singing, dancing or just talking.

The platforms of the London Underground stations became a popular place to shelter for many Londoners. These were deeper underground than any of the shelters. People felt safer in the tube stations and they were also far quieter than any of the other shelters. You could hardly hear the noise of the bombs dropping.

## THINGS TO DO

**1** At bedtime during the war you would have had to leave all your clothes out ready in case you had to go quickly to your air raid shelter in the night. Make a list of what you would have to get ready to take to your shelter. Remember you might have to spend the rest of the night there and not be able to sleep – how would you occupy yourself?

**2** WORD FIT
Try to fit the words on the left into the grid. There is only one way for them to fit.

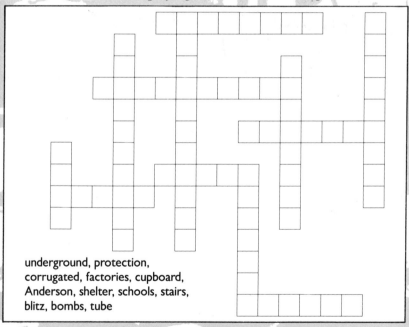

underground, protection, corrugated, factories, cupboard, Anderson, shelter, schools, stairs, blitz, bombs, tube

---

**14th February 1941**

German troops specially trained for fighting in the desert and led by General Rommel land in North Africa. They have come to help the Italians who have lost many battles.

**1st March 1941**

Bulgaria, under threat of attack from Germany, agrees to join the AXIS powers and to be occupied by German soldiers.

**11th March 1941**

President Roosevelt of the U.S.A. signs an agreement to allow Britain to have American weapons without having to pay for them until the war is over. It is known as the *Lease and Lend Bill* and helps Britain greatly as she has spent millions of pounds on the war so far.

# ON DUTY

While most people were safe in their shelters during an air raid, or asleep in their beds on quiet nights, there were large numbers of people on duty every night. Police, fire services, ambulance teams with their doctors and nurses, and the rescue workers who dug people out of damaged buildings all had work to do during an air raid. When called they would have to leave their shelters or protected bases and go out among the falling bombs.

## A.R.P. WARDENS

Other people with a lot to do during an air raid were the Air Raid Protection (A.R.P.) wardens. These were local people who looked after a small area – usually just a few streets. They made sure that everyone followed the Blackout rules and they attended the scene of a bomb explosion as soon as it happened. They had then to inform a central Control who organized ambulance, fire and rescue services when needed. If the incident was not too severe the A.R.P. warden would be able to cope and give simple first aid. In more severe situations, the warden had to keep people calm and tell them where to go if their homes had been bombed out.

A.R.P. wardens also had the dangerous task of making the first investigations into reports of unexploded bombs and calling the bomb disposal squad where necessary.

For most A.R.P. wardens this was a part-time job, although there were a few full-time wardens who would keep an eye on the neighbourhood during the day, as well as night. Part-time wardens often had full-time day jobs and then spent many of their days off, evenings and nights on duty.

## HOME GUARD

Another group of people who spent their spare time on duty were the *Home Guard*. The Home Guard started in May 1940 as the *Local Defence Volunteers* (L.D.V.) but Churchill soon suggested that Home Guard was a better name.

Many of the first men to volunteer to join were old soldiers from the First World War and even earlier wars. The age of the men who joined up soon led to the Home Guard becoming jokingly known as "Dad's Army".

In the first few months after the Home Guard was formed they were given no uniforms, only armbands with L.D.V. stamped on them, and no weapons. They would be seen marching along with

pitch - forks, old shotguns, broomsticks and anything else which would do as a weapon. However, the enthusiasm of these men and radio and newspaper stories helped make

---

| 17th March 1941 | 17th April 1941 | 27th April 1941 |
|---|---|---|
| The government in Britain announces a scheme to register all 20 and 21-year-old women to do Essential War Work. Many other women are being encouraged to volunteer to take men's jobs so that men can be free to join the fighting. | Yugoslavia which has been fighting an invasion by German troops is defeated and occupied. | The German Army which had come to help the Italians in fighting the Greeks, wins the battle and occupies Greece. |

the Germans think they were a proper fighting force.

By the middle of 1941 the Home Guard had changed greatly from its early "Dad's Army" style. All the men over 60 years old were forced to leave. Uniforms and proper weapons were issued and the Home Guard became organized like the full-time army with privates, sergeants and other army ranks. Their job, as always, was to defend Britain against any invasion. The invasion never came and their hours of duty were spent helping out in air raids and practising fighting skills.

## WOMEN ON DUTY

Many women had wanted to join the Home Guard but the government would not let them. They thought that the country would feel the war was being lost if Britain had to use women to do the fighting! This was despite the fact that a number of women were already responsible for firing the anti-aircraft guns which shot down enemy planes. In the end thousands of women formed themselves into the *Women's Home Defence Movement* and arranged their own training in fighting and the use of weapons.

Every night and during air raids there would be many women on duty. Many A.R.P. wardens were female and they had the same responsibilities as male wardens. Nearly all the ambulances, driven through the bombing, were driven by women. Each ambulance would carry a team of three nurses, usually women, and a doctor who was usually a man. People bombed out of their homes would go to rest centres staffed by women volunteers from organizations such as the W.V.S. (Women's Voluntary Service).

## THINGS TO DO

**1** Design a poster, using only three colours, to be put in a work place, to encourage men to join the Home Guard.

**2** Before the war Air Raid Protection (A.R.P.) was known as Civil Defence. There is a Civil Defence in Britain nowadays. Find out all you can about it.

| 11th May 1941 | 24th May 1941 | 27th May 1941 |
|---|---|---|
| London suffers its worst night of bombing. 550 planes drop hundreds of explosive bombs and 100,000 incendiary (fire) bombs. The Germans say it is revenge for the heavy bombing of German towns. | HMS *Hood*, said to be the Royal Navy's finest battleship, is blown up when a shell from the German battleship *Bismarck* hits her weapons' store. | The *Bismarck*, which the German Navy claimed was unsinkable, is sunk after being attacked by Royal Navy ships which chased her for 1,750 miles after she destroyed HMS *Hood*. |

# RATIONING

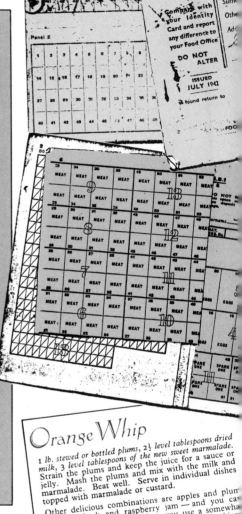

## FOOD COSTS LIVES

In 1939, as now, much of Britain's food was *imported,* that is brought in from other countries around the world. From the very beginning of the war people realized that food would have to be rationed so that everyone would have a fair share of what was available. All imported food was brought in by ship. As the German Navy tried to sink the ships this meant that everything that was imported put sailors' lives at risk, so only the really necessary items were brought in.

## RATIONS

Food rationing in Britain began on 8th January 1940. The system of rationing in Britain was quite simple. Everyone was given a ration book and had to register with a grocer and a butcher where they would exchange the coupons in the ration book and the necessary money. People could not buy ration food anywhere except the shops they had registered at.

Fresh food such as fish, bread, offal (liver, kidney, hearts etc) and fruit were not rationed but

*Average rations per person per week in Britain:*

4oz (100g) cheese
4oz (100g) bacon
2oz (50g)  butter
2oz (50g)  cooking fat
2oz (50g)  margarine
8oz (225g) sugar
4oz (100g) jam
3oz (75g)  sweets
2oz (50g)  tea (adults only)
approximately ¾lb (350g) of minced beef or meat of equivalent value
1 fresh egg (3 for children)
3 eggs as dried egg powder
7 pints of milk for children under 5
3½ pints of milk for school age children (most of whom also had school milk)
1 pint's worth of dried milk

were often in such short supply that they could only be bought by queuing outside the shop for hours. Some foods, like bananas, were almost never seen and any oranges that were in the shops were reserved for children. A few foods such as potatoes, carrots and other home-grown

### Orange Whip

1 lb. stewed or bottled plums, 2½ level tablespoons dried milk, 3 level tablespoons of the new sweet marmalade. Strain the plums and keep the juice for a sauce or jelly. Mash the plums and mix with the milk and marmalade. Beat well. Serve in individual dishes topped with marmalade or custard.

Other delicious combinations are apples and plum jam; rhubarb and raspberry jam — and you can think of many others. When you use a somewhat colourless fruit it is best to combine it with a red jam. These fruit whips are very easy to make and gre favourites at children's parties.

### Macaroons

1 tablespoon water, 1 oz. margarine, 1 teaspoon rat or almond essence, 2 oz. sugar, 2 oz. soya flour. Melt margarine in water, add essence and su then soya flour. Turn on to a board and knead Roll mixture into balls, flatten slightly and bake moderate oven for 20 minutes, till golden brow

ISSUED BY THE MINISTRY OF

| 1st June 1941 | 22nd June 1941 | 4th July 1941 |
|---|---|---|
| Clothes rationing introduced in Britain. Everyone is allowed 60 coupons per year. | In a plan codenamed *Barbarossa,* Germany invades Russia – trying the Blitzkrieg methods that were so successful in defeating other, smaller countries. | Coal rationing begins in Britain. |

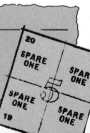

vegetables were not rationed and could be bought quite easily. Through the Ministry of Food, the government ran adverts to encourage people to eat as much of these foods as possible.

## UNDER THE COUNTER

*Under the counter* became a famous phrase during the war. Shopkeepers would keep supplies of unrationed food off the shelves and only sell it to regular customers.

The shopkeeper sold this food at prices fixed by the government, unlike people selling on the *black market* where goods were sold for very high prices. Most ordinary people did buy things under the counter but it was really only the wealthy who could afford to buy on the black market.

It was strictly against the law to sell things for more than the government's fixed price. This was to make sure that everyone

# Potatoes are part of the battle

## OLD MONEY

In 1939 the system of money was different to the decimal system we have now.

| Old Money | | Our money |
|---|---|---|
| £1 20s (shillings) | | 100p |
| 2s (shillings) | | 10p |
| 12d (pennies) | 1s (shilling) | 5p |
| 6d (pennies) | | 2½p |
| 1d (penny) | Just under | ½p |

Prices in old money were written like this:

1/- one shilling or 5p in our money

2/10 two shillings and ten pence or 14p in today's money

£1.10.10d one pound, ten shillings and 10 pence or £1.54 today.

could afford to buy their weekly ration.

## EXTRA RATIONS

Apart from queuing and buying under the counter or on the black market, there were two other ways to get extra food. One was to grow it yourself, and nearly every garden in Britain was dug up and planted with fruit and vegetables. The other way was a different type of rationing which

began in November 1941. It gave people a choice of how they spent extra rations.

As well as the weekly ration, people were allowed 16 "points" (later 20) per month with which to buy luxury-type foods such as

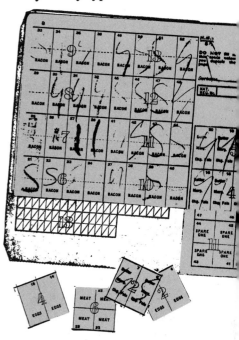

biscuits, dried fruit, breakfast cereals and tinned food. Very often some foods on the points system were not available and people would just have to have whatever was available.

## HELPFUL HINTS

Magazines and newspapers were full of hints on how to make food

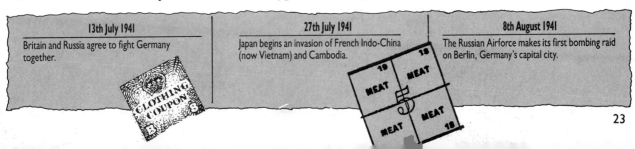

| 13th July 1941 | 27th July 1941 | 8th August 1941 |
|---|---|---|
| Britain and Russia agree to fight Germany together. | Japan begins an invasion of French Indo-China (now Vietnam) and Cambodia. | The Russian Airforce makes its first bombing raid on Berlin, Germany's capital city. |

go further and make meals more interesting. There were also ideas for substitutes for foods you could not buy or which were in short supply:

- A sort of coffee could be made from ground acorns.
- Marmalade could be made from carrots.
- Grated raw beetroot was used to replace dried fruit in cakes.
- "Banana" sandwiches could be made with cooled, cooked parsnips flavoured with artificial banana flavouring.

As the weekly sweet ration was the equivalent of one Mars Bar, children were encouraged to learn to like eating raw carrots instead of sweets.

## Count your Coupons

Lots of recipes appeared in newspapers and magazines, some in adverts for products such as Oxo and Bovril, others in adverts from the Ministry of Food. These recipes encouraged people to use foods that they would never have dreamt of eating before the war. Things such as sheep's heads, raw sprouts and cabbage in salads, dried egg and all sorts of peculiar looking fish.

One of the most interesting facts about people's eating habits during the war is that they made everyone far healthier than either before or afterwards. Before the war people did not have enough of the right food to eat and after the war people ate too much rich food.

## RATIONING IN GERMANY

The German people were already experiencing food

## DIG FOR VICTORY

One way in which nearly everyone in the country was involved in work on the land was through the *Dig for Victory* Campaign. This encouraged people to grow as much of their own food as possible. Those who did not have a garden could have an allotment. Any spare land, even the moat of the Tower of London was dug over to provide allotments. The campaign also encouraged people to pick the fruit, vegetables and fungi from hedgerows and woods. So teams of children and their mothers would pick dandelion leaves, stinging nettles, blackberries and crab apples. These teams picked enough rosehips to supply all the rosehip syrup needed through the war.

rationing at the beginning of the war, but as it progressed, the farms and workers of German occupied countries helped keep Germany supplied with food. It was not until towards the end of the war, when Germany began losing, that the German people had to suffer severe rationing.

## A GERMAN SOLDIER'S RATIONS

A German soldier going on leave for 14 days would be given 450g (1lb) sausages, 450g (1lb) bacon and a !oaf for the journey home. He would also take with him a ration card allowing him to buy the following for his 14 day stay:

10lbs (4.5kg) bread and cake

2lbs (900g) meat

1lb (450g) butter

1lb (450g) food like pasta and rice

½lb (225g) jam

½lb (225g) vegetables

1lb (450g) sugar

½lb (225g) coffee mixture

½lb (225g) pure coffee

2oz (50g) tea

4oz (100g) nuts

4oz (100g) chocolate

2 eggs

4 pieces of cheese

| 1st September 1941 |
| --- |
| American President Roosevelt promises to do "everything in our power to crush Hitler and his Nazi forces". They still will not join the fighting. |

| 17th September 1941 |
| --- |
| The British government orders that potatoes be sold at 1d (½p) a pound so that people will eat more of them. |

| 24th September 1941 |
| --- |
| The Germans are fighting just outside the Russian city of Leningrad, having made great advances in the war against Russia. |

# Feeding FIVE on £3·10d a Week

## CORNED BEEF PIE

3 rations of corned beef (6d. worth).
1 cup finely shredded raw vegetables (carrots, potato, leek, swede, etc.).
1 Stock Cube.
1 teaspoonful chopped parsley.
Small piece fat.
Short crust pastry (6 ozs. flour, 3 ozs. fat).
1 dessertspoon flour.

Melt the fat in a small pan and lightly fry the vegetable. Stir in the flour and cook a few minutes. Add 1 cup of cold water and the crumbled stock cube. Stir until thickened. Draw off the heat, add cubed meat, parsley and seasoning to taste. Line a small plate with pastry and spread it with the meat mixture. Cover with pastry, seal the edges and decorate with pastry leaves. Bake in a moderate oven 30 minutes.                    4 servings.

potatoes for
's Sunday's joint"

ways with the new

T FISH

## THINGS TO DO

**1** Work out how much food your whole family would have had each week by adding up the ration for each person in your family. See if you can plan a week's menus for your family using these rations.

Try to find out how much your family's wartime rations would cost at today's prices and compare that with how much your family now spends on food.

**2** Try to cook some of the recipes mentioned in this section. Get an adult to help you if you need it!

**3** Design and make some coupons for a shop of your own – remember paper was scarce. You will need different types of food. You could then run your own shop, deciding how much each coupon will buy.

**4** Write about some of the foods you would have missed during rationing.

**5** *How to make Rosehip Syrup*
Get an adult's help if you need it. Collect 1 kg. rosehips. Top and tail and wash them. Put them into 750cl of water. Bring them to the boil and simmer for 15 minutes. Rub the hips through a sieve and mix with 500 grammes of caster sugar. Put this mixture back into a pan and bring to the boil, then allow to simmer for about 15 minutes. Allow to cool slightly then pour into sterilized jars. Seal and cover. Keep the rosehip syrup in a dark cupboard. It can be used straightaway and will keep for 3 or 4 months. Take one teaspoon a day or you can dilute the syrup with water as a drink.

| **26th September 1941** | **4th October 1941** | **5th October 1941** |
| --- | --- | --- |
| The RAF fly to help the Russians defend Leningrad. | The people of Norway are warned by the Germans that food supplies will be cut if they do not stop resisting German rule. | Russian bombers fly to help the Resistance Movement in Yugoslavia. |

# MAKE DO AND MEND

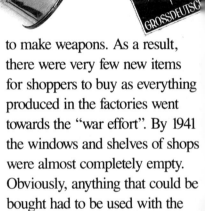

During the war the government's first priority was to make weapons with which to fight. For this they needed tons of metal and other materials. Importing these materials from abroad was hazardous as, just as with the importing of food, it put the lives of sailors at risk for their ships were in constant danger of being attacked and sunk. The government therefore looked for another way of providing these much needed materials and decided to *salvage* them from everyday objects.

The WVS (Women's Voluntary Service) organized teams of women and children to go from house to house collecting as much metal as possible as well as other useful materials.

Examples of materials salvaged to go towards the "war effort".
Scraps of rubber
Saucepans
Kettles
Tin baths
Old tin cans
Toothpaste tubes
Animal bones
Rags
Waste-paper

All this material was used to make tanks, planes, bullets, ships, guns, bombs and other fighting equipment. By 1944 the women and children of Britain had collected so much that 50,000 tanks could have been built from the metal alone.

In addition to the material salvaged, all new metal and rubber produced had to be used

to make weapons. As a result, there were very few new items for shoppers to buy as everything produced in the factories went towards the "war effort". By 1941 the windows and shelves of shops were almost completely empty. Obviously, anything that could be bought had to be used with the utmost care so that nothing was wasted.

## Is YOUR home helping to build a destroyer?

Save **FUEL** for **BATTLE**

ISSUED BY THE MINISTRY OF FUEL AND POWE

| ITEMS IN SHORT SUPPLY | |
|---|---|
| Crockery | Furniture |
| Cutlery | Floor polish |
| Shoes | Buckets |
| Ladies' stockings | Curtains |
| Towels | Pillows |
| Blankets | Toys |

---

| 20th October 1941 | 3rd November 1941 | 13th November 1941 |
|---|---|---|
| The Russian government moves to a town 500 miles east of Moscow, as the capital city is under threat of being occupied by German soldiers. | The U.S. Ambassador in Tokyo warns President Roosevelt that Japan may attack the U.S.A. | A torpedo from an Italian U-boat sinks HMS *Ark Royal*, the British Navy's largest aircraft carrier. |

# GS

## *y eggs"*

In June 1940 the government followed the German example and introduced a system of clothes rationing. Again this was because materials were in short supply and all the factories were involved in making weapons. As a result people had few new clothes throughout the war.

## SOAP AND WATER

By the middle of 1942 soap was rationed to 3oz (75g) per person per week. This was not only to be used for washing but also to keep clothes and houses clean too.

Even water had to be used sparingly. This was because the coal normally used to heat water and homes had to be saved to power the weapons factories.

• No one was allowed more than 5 inches (13 cms) of water in their *weekly* bath. Even the king and queen had a line painted on their bath to show the 5 inch mark.

### Now that Soap is Rationed

Frieze cloth: beautifully gored from waist to give full flare: high neck line with smart stand collar; front belt Navy, Brown, and Green 35/9

---

| 30th November 1941 | 6th December 1941 | 7th December 1941 |
|---|---|---|
| The Eighth Army, a mixture of British and Commonwealth troops, have had some success against the German and Italian armies in the deserts of North Africa. The men of the Eighth Army are becoming known as the "Desert Rats". | President Roosevelt makes an appeal to Emperor Hirohito of Japan to try to avoid a war between the two countries. | Japanese planes attack the US Navy Pacific fleet at its base in Pearl Harbour, Hawaii. U.S.A. and Japan are now at War. |

27

UNITY

FURNITURE POLISH

SHOW MOTHER

WHAT YOU CAN DO

## HOUSEHOLD ITEMS

As many household items could not be replaced during the war, the only solution was to *make do and mend*.

Magazines, newspapers, radio broadcasts and special classes all showed women how to mend things around the house and make whatever they had last longer.

Here is a list of some of the hints given:

- How to patch worn towels
- How to make new clothes from old
- How to unravel old woollens and knit new ones
- How to make soap last longer
- How to make an old drawer into a baby's cot
- How to repair and take care of shoes
- How to make polish and face creams.

Most of the people giving this advice overlooked the fact that in many cases it was impossible to find the ingredients or materials needed for all this *make do and mend*. Glue for repair to breakages, needles and threads for knitting and sewing, rubber for patching bicycle tyres or repairing shoes — all these were in as short supply as the items they were supposed to mend!

## THINGS TO DO

**1** Collect ends and bits of soap and try either or both of the following recipes. Get an adult to help or supervise if you need it:

a) SOAP JELLY: When you have enough scraps of soap to fill a cup, cut it up fairly small and mix it with 1/3 pint of boiling water. Stir until the soap has dissolved. Pour into a jar or pot and leave until cold. You can add perfume to the mixture if you wish.

b) BAR OF SOAP: Put some scraps of soap, together with a few drops of glycerine into an old cup or bowl. Place the cup or bowl over a pan of boiling water (just as you would do to melt a bar of chocolate). Leave until the soap becomes soft. When cool, knead into a ball then shape into a bar of soap.

**2** Unravel the wool from an old woollen. Wind the wool round something like a large book or the back of a chair. Try to pull it tight. When you have a fairly large skein of wool tie it round so that it will not slip out of the skein while you wash it and then hang it out to dry. When the wool is dry you can knit it into something else. You might try knitting squares to make a blanket for Oxfam.

**3** Design a poster to encourage people to save and not waste anything.

**4** Try to interview someone who was running a home during the war. Make a list of questions to ask them (not just about rationing). You can record your interview on audio or video cassette if possible.

| 8th December 1941 | 25th December 1941 | 26th January 1942 |
|---|---|---|
| Britain declares war on Japan. | Hong Kong surrenders to Japan. Since the attack on Pearl Harbour Japanese troops have attacked with great success in Malaya, Singapore, the Phillipines and Burma. | Ships filled with American soldiers (GIs) land in Northern Ireland. They are the first Americans to join in the fighting in Europe. |

# AT SEA

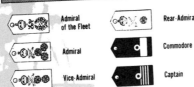

The Navy's role in the war was twofold:

1. The *Merchant Navy* carried food and raw materials to Britain from abroad.
2. The *Royal Navy* were the fighting ships involved in sea battles.

Both these services saw action throughout the world's oceans, but the two most important areas were the Atlantic and Pacific Oceans.

## THE ATLANTIC OCEAN

Large numbers of merchant ships crossed the Atlantic Ocean from the U.S.A., carrying supplies to Britain. The German Navy had twenty-eight *U-boats* (submarines) at the beginning of the war and even these few boats

| | | | |
|---|---|---|---|
| Admiral of the Fleet | | Rear-Admiral | |
| Admiral | | Commodore | |
| Vice-Admiral | | Captain | |

were very successful in sinking large numbers of supply ships crossing the ocean. This success encouraged the Germans to build more U-boats and for a large part of the war they were a major threat to shipping right across the Atlantic.

In order to protect merchant ships from attack by U-boats lots of ships joined together to form *convoys*. These convoys were protected by Royal Navy warships and together they could cross the ocean much more safely. In response, the German Navy arranged for the U-boats to group together to attack the convoys. These groups of U-boats became known as *wolf-packs* because like wolves they hunted together at night. For nearly two years the attacks by the wolf-packs were very successful in sinking supplies headed for Britain.

## AIRCRAFT AT SEA

By the middle of 1942 Britain had found that the best way to fight the U-boats was *from the air*. The U-boats were tracked underwater by radar and when they surfaced, as they had to do quite often to recharge their batteries, planes would drop bombs on them.

At the end of the war it was discovered that Germany was developing plans for U-boats that could stay underwater for much longer and so have less chance of being destroyed.

The sea battles in the Second World War showed for the first time just how important planes were to the Royal Navy. Like U-boats, many of Germany's surface ships were destroyed or disabled by attacks from planes. The German Navy never had a large number of surface ships and by November 1944 all those she did have were out of action.

| 15th February 1942 | 10th March 1942 | 22nd March 1942 |
|---|---|---|
| Singapore surrenders to the Japanese. The Allies have lost an extremely important Naval base in the Indian and Pacific Oceans. | Figures show that so far Britain has spent £9,050 million pounds on the war. | The BBC broadcast the first of its daily news bulletins in morse code to the French Resistance fighters. |

## A SAILOR'S JOB

Life for merchant seamen on the convoys was very hard. When Russia joined the war Britain and the U.S.A. started to send supplies to Russia's North coast. This meant journeys through freezing seas with ice everywhere on deck. Apart from the difficulties with rough seas and weather conditions, the sailors in the convoys were under constant threat of being sunk by German U-boats and had no way of defending themselves.

## SEA BATTLES

In addition to protecting the convoys of merchant ships carrying supplies, the Royal Navy was involved in a number of sea battles with German surface ships. One of their most notable successes was the sinking of the *Bismarck,* a ship which the Germans had boasted was unsinkable. After sinking the Royal Navy's HMS *Hood,* the *Bismarck* was chased and destroyed by Royal Navy warships.

# THE PACIFIC OCEAN

The battle in the Atlantic Ocean was important to the survival of the British people. Without the food and raw materials from the supply ships, they could not have continued to fight. However, in the Pacific Ocean the battles

# NIGHT PATROL
### Alan Ross

We sail at dusk, the red moon
Like a paper lantern setting fire
To our wake. Headlands disappear,
Muffled in their own velvet.

Docks dwindle, rubbed out by mists,
Their cranes, like drunks, askew
Over jetties. Coal is unloaded
Under blue arc-lights.

Turning south, the mapped moon
Swings between masts, our aerials
Swollen and lurching. The bag
Of sea squirts black and sooty.

Flashes of gunfire, perhaps lightning,
Straddle our progress, a convoy
Of hearses. The bow-waves of gunboats
Sew us together, helplessly idling.

The watch changes, and changes
Again. We edge through a minefield,
Real or imaginary. The speed of a convoy
Is the speed of the slowest ship.

No one speaks, it might be a funeral.
Altering course, the moon congeals
On a new bearing. The telegraph rings,
And, at speed now, clouds grow visible.

We're on our own, making for harbour.
In tangerine light we sniff greenness,
Tremble like racehorses. Soon minesweepers
Pass us, continuing our business.

| 28th March 1942 | 16th April 1942 | 18th April 1942 |
| --- | --- | --- |
| The RAF begins an all out attack to try to destroy Germany's weapons factories. | The Island of Malta is awarded the George Cross in recognition of the "heroism and devotion" of its people after more than 2,000 air raids, both day and night. | American B25 bombers raid Tokyo, Japan's capital, and several other cities. The planes have been launched from the aircraft carrier *Hornet,* as there are no land bases near enough. |

were fought for a different reason. Here, the aim was to take control of the hundreds of islands — small and large — and to push the enemy back. Merchant ships were rarely involved as the main fighting took place between warships.

Just as in the Atlantic, planes played an important part in attacking enemy ships in the Pacific. In the Battle of the Coral Sea in 1942, the U.S. and Japanese navies fought a five day battle and yet the ships of either side never even saw one another. Instead, the battle was fought by planes launched from each navy's aircraft carriers.

## WRENS

The war changed women's lives considerably as in many cases it gave them an opportunity to train for jobs previously only held by men. At sea, the *Women's Royal Naval Service* (WRNS), or "Wrens" as they became known, played a very important part in the war.

Before the war Wrens did mainly clerical and cleaning jobs, but then in order for the men to be free to join the fighting ships, some women became ship engineers. They learned how to build, repair and service not only the ships but vital weapons such as torpedoes. Other Wrens worked in the central control offices of Navy Command where they were involved in the crucial task of plotting routes of both enemy and friendly ships and planes. While women were not allowed to be involved in the actual fighting, some Wrens had jobs as radio operators on warships and therefore were at the same risk as men.

 Commander   Lieutenant

## MINES

Early on in the war, ships of all types were sunk by a terrifying new weapon used by the German Navy — the *Magnetic Mine*. Ordinary mines were known about — they floated in the sea so that when a ship bumped into them they would explode. The Magnetic Mine was a new idea, because a ship did not even have to touch it to be destroyed. The mine simply exploded when the metal hull of a ship passed by setting off magnetic signals which completed an electrical circuit inside the mine.

It was later discovered that the hull of a ship could be demagnetized by running an electric cable round the underwater hull. Then the magnetic mines would not be triggered off when the ship sailed near them.

## THINGS TO DO

**1** Every Navy has its own flag. Find out what the flags of all the navies involved in the Second World War looked like and make drawings of them.

**2** During the Second World War women in the navy, airforce and army were not allowed to be involved in the actual fighting. Do you think that in a war today women and men should do exactly the same jobs?

**3** Try to write a poem of your own about ships in wartime. You could write it as if you were a sailor on a ship or as a person on shore waiting for a ship.

| 24th April 1942 | 8th May 1942 | 30th May 1942 |
|---|---|---|
| The Luftwaffe are attacking smaller, less well defended towns like Exeter, Bath, Norwich and York in revenge for the heavy bombing of German towns by RAF planes trying to destroy weapons factories. | The Battle of the Coral Sea has ended. In a sea battle lasting five days the US and Japanese navies launched planes from their aircraft carriers which fought with the planes and ships of the other side, but the ships never even saw one another. | The RAF drops 2,000 tons of bombs from 1,000 bomber planes in a raid on Cologne which they claim has destroyed more than 200 factories. |

# PROGRESS OF THE WAR

KEY

■ Land areas where fighting was taking place

■ Sea areas where naval battles were taking place

■ Areas whose people were involved in the fighting

**THE WORLD AT WAR DEC 1941–AUG 1945**

Although the war is always called the Second World War, for the first two years it did not really involve most of the world. It was mainly a war in Europe, although there were soldiers from British colonies, (now Commonwealth Countries) such as India, New Zealand, Australia, Canada and the West Indies, involved in the fighting. Many of the Commonwealth troops became members of the Eighth Army and were known as the "Desert Rats" because nearly all their fighting was in the difficult desert conditions of North Africa.

## WAR IN NORTH AFRICA

Mussolini, Italy's leader, tried to take control of North Africa in the summer of 1940. This would give Italy control of the Mediterranean Sea. All the European countries surrounding the Mediterranean, except Spain which was not involved in the war, belonged to the *Axis* powers.

## THE AXIS POWERS

GERMANY ITALY JAPAN

Some countries, such as Bulgaria, and Hungary joined the Axis powers after threats from Germany. Other countries, such as France, Denmark, Belgium and Yugoslavia were occupied after fierce fighting.

The Italian soldiers fighting in the deserts of North Africa were joined by the Germans, led by Field Marshal Rommel, in April 1941. For the next year the Eighth Army lost many battles to the Axis powers.

| 7th June 1942 | 21st June 1942 | 6th July 1942 |
|---|---|---|
| After a four day battle, off the coast of Midway Island, the Japanese Navy is beaten by attacks from US Navy ships and planes. It is America's first victory in the war against Japan. | The Eighth Army loses the port of Tobruk in North Africa to Field Marshal Rommel and the German Army. About 25,000 Allied soldiers are taken prisoner. | The Eighth Army has beaten back a German attack at El Alamein. It is the Allies' first success against the Germans in North Africa. |

In the Mediterranean the only bases Britain had were Gibraltar at the southern tip of Spain, and the island of Malta. Malta suffered terrible bombing but was never defeated. The whole island was awarded a medal, the George Cross, in recognition of the hardship endured and bravery of its people.

However, the British forces, led by General Montgomery ("Monty" as he was known to the soldiers) won an important battle at El Alamein in 1942. Over the next six months the Eighth Army gradually won the war in the desert until in May 1943 the Axis armies were defeated and over quarter of a million prisoners taken.

## WAR IN RUSSIA

On 22nd June 1941 Germany invaded Russia, despite having signed an agreement with Stalin not to attack. Hitler wanted to destroy the communist system in Russia. He also wanted to

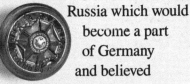

take over a large area of Russia which would become a part of Germany and believed with this extra land Germany would be impossible to beat.

The war in Russia was terrible. The Russian people suffered huge loss of life. In one battle alone, that for the city of Stalingrad, the Russians lost more people than the Americans did in the whole war. For the German soldiers too the Russian war was dreadful. They had to fight in severe winter conditions. For months the temperature would not rise above freezing. The wintry conditions also meant it was difficult to keep the German troops supplied with food and weapons but Hitler was determined not to give up.

## WAR IN THE FAR EAST

When Japan attacked the United States Navy at Pearl

Harbour on 7th December 1941 America finally entered the war on the side of the *Allies*.

## THE ALLIES

BRITAIN AND THE COMMONWEALTH (including Australia, Canada, India, New Zealand and the West Indies)
RUSSIA
THE UNITED STATES OF AMERICA

Fighting now spread to the countries bordering, and the islands in, the Pacific Ocean. American, British and Commonwealth troops had to learn to fight the Japanese in the jungle conditions of places like Burma and Malaya.

## NEUTRAL COUNTRIES

Some countries refused to become involved in the war. In Europe, Southern Ireland, Sweden and Switzerland never took sides. None of the countries in South America were actively involved in the war nor were a number of African countries. Of course, both Axis and Allies always accused these countries of helping the other side but it is difficult to prove any of these claims.

IMPERIAL WAR MUSEUM

### 15th July 1942
The RAF carries out its first daylight raid on the main industrial area in Germany in the Ruhr valley. A new plane, the Lancaster bomber, is used in these raids.

### 19th August 1942
British and Canadian troops raid the occupied French port of Dieppe. After fierce fighting the Allies destroy a large number of tanks and boats but lose 1,500 prisoners to the Germans. The Allies claim this was a practice for a proper invasion of Europe.

### 18th September 1942
There is fighting in the Russian city of Stalingrad between the German and Russian Armies. Every day the German soldiers advance, only to be beaten back at night.

# JAPAN ATTACKS U.S.A.

In the 1930s, Japan occupied large parts of China, which provided her with extra food, raw materials, and a market for her goods.

The U.S.A. – the major power in the Pacific – felt threatened by Japan and stopped trading with her. Starved of oil, Japan planned to destroy the U.S. Pacific fleet. Without U.S. interference, she could take over more territory and safeguard her own oil supply.

On 7th December 1941, Japanese planes attacked the U.S. Naval base at Pearl Harbour in Hawaii. However, only a few ships were lost.

## THINGS TO DO

**1** Find out what the flags of the main countries involved looked like during World War Two. Make a wall chart showing the flags of the Axis powers on one side and the flags of the Allies on the other. You could also find out and include on the chart the symbols each country used, e.g. the swastika for Germany.

## 2 AXIS ACROSTIC

**CLUES ACROSS**
1. One of the countries that joined the Axis after threats from Hitler.
2. This country was invaded by Germany on the same day in May 1940 that Prime Minister Chamberlain resigned.
3. Britain's ally at the very beginning of the war until it was occupied by Germany.
4. A tiny European country invaded at the same time as No. 2.
5. The country that attacked U.S.A. at Pearl Harbour.
6. A country bordering Germany in the North which was occupied by Hitler's armies in 1940.
7. Country led by Mussolini and his Fascist party.

**DOWN**
What country appears in the shaded area?

## 3 ALLIES ACROSTIC

**CLUES ACROSS**
1. Place at the entrance to the Mediterranean Sea that was an important base for the Allies.
2. Commonwealth country in the southern hemisphere.
3. Commonwealth country that has an ocean named after it.
4. The name of a group of islands in the Caribbean Sea.
5. The initials by which the United States of America are known.
6. Another name for the U.S.S.R.
7. A Commonwealth country in North America.

**DOWN**
What country appears in the shaded area?

## 2 THE AXIS POWERS

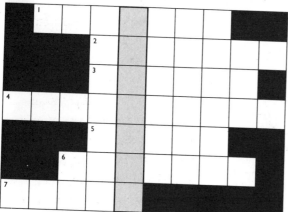

## 3 THE ALLIES

| 8th October 1942 | 31st October 1942 | 4th November 1942 |
|---|---|---|
| In Norway the resistance to German occupation has led to severe laws, arrests and executions. | Canterbury is bombed by the Luftwaffe. Bravery by firemen and ARP wardens save the cathedral buildings. | General Montgomery's Eighth Army wins the battle of El Alamein for the Allies. Rommel's troops and panzers (tanks) are retreating. |

# AIRFORCE

The Royal Air Force (RAF) was only twenty-one years old when war broke out in 1939. It had been formed out of the Royal Flying Corps at the end of the First World War in 1918. During the First War only a small amount of fighting had been done in the air. In contrast, in the Second World War the airforces of the countries involved were of great importance in the fighting and the crews of every plane had a very dangerous job to do.

## BOMBING RUNS

One of the airforce's main jobs was the bombing of towns. In the air a bomber plane would have a crew of about six men — a pilot who flew the plane and a navigator who made sure the plane followed the proper route. The other men on board would be responsible for dropping the bombs and using the plane's machine guns to fight off any attacks by enemy aircraft.

Using the instruments on the plane and the navigator's skill in following aerial maps and photographs, the plane would be flown to the target area where the bombs would be dropped. Occasionally instead of dropping

| | |
|---|---|
| Marshal of the Royal Air Force | |
| Air Chief Marshal | |
| Air Marshal | |
| Air Vice-Marshal | |
| Air Commodore | |
| Group-Captain | |
| Wing-Commander | |
| Squadron-Leader | |
| Flight-Lieutenant | |
| Flying Officer | |

bombs the plane would drop propaganda leaflets telling people on the ground that they should surrender.

Each flight brought danger and the aircrew knew they could possibly be fired on from the ground by anti-aircraft guns, or attacked by fighter planes from the enemy airforce. Low flying aircraft also risked becoming entangled in the cables of barrage balloons.

## BARRAGE BALLOONS

These were groups of huge gas-filled balloons which floated in the air and were tied to the ground by cables. They would stop low flying aircraft by trapping them in their cables.

Most bombing of cities was done under cover of darkness which made the planes more difficult to see and shoot down, but some raids did take place in daylight. Most of the daylight bombing of Germany was carried out by the American Airforce.

The bombing raids on Germany cost the lives of more than 150,000 RAF and U.S. Airforce men and 600,000 German civilians.

## THE AIRFORCE AND THE NAVY

Planes were important in other areas of fighting, particularly at sea where aircraft were used to attack and sink both U-boats and surface ships. Sometimes planes had to take off and land on aircraft carriers while at sea. When attacking a ship a plane was at risk of being shot down by the anti-aircraft guns onboard.

## KAMIKAZE

The Japanese Navy found that U.S. Navy ships were really too well protected for an attacking plane to do much damage, so they devised a deadly way of using their planes to great effect. A pilot would volunteer to die for his country by aiming a plane loaded with explosives at the weakest part of an enemy ship. The Japanese pilot would die as

| 7th November 1942 | 26th November 1942 | 17th December 1942 |
|---|---|---|
| 140,000 US soldiers land in North Africa in an invasion by ship and plane. The US troops plan to move east to trap Rommel's Army between themselves and Montgomery's Eighth Army. | The Russian Red Army has begun to win the battle against the Germans in Stalingrad. | The governments of the U.S.A., Russia and Britain condemn the Germans for carrying out Hitler's intention to exterminate the Jewish people in Europe. |

the plane exploded, damaging or sinking the target ship. These men were known as *Kamikaze* pilots.

Kamikaze was the name of a wind in a Japanese legend, which was sent by the gods to destroy the enemies of Japan.

## DISPOSABLE PLANES!

Not all convoys could be accompanied by an aircraft carrier. So sometimes merchant ships would carry planes. The plane would be catapulted into the air from the ship to patrol the sea, looking for enemy ships or U-boats. The deck was too small for the plane to land, so the pilot would parachute into the sea when the fuel ran out and be picked up by a ship in the convoy. The plane would be left to crash and sink.

## THE AIRFORCE AND THE ARMY

Throughout the war there were many instances of planes being used to attack or give cover to troops on the ground, for example, at Dunkirk, where the Luftwaffe tried to shoot the soldiers on the beaches, while the RAF tried to protect them. Planes also played an important part in the war in North Africa and in the jungles of the Far East.

Aircraft were also used to carry spies who would parachute into enemy country. Sometimes only one man or woman would be dropped. Other times thousands of men would parachute from hundreds of planes as part of an invasion force. Hitler used soldiers parachuting into a country as part of his Blitzkrieg and usually they

were the first soldiers to invade the country. The Allies also made use of parachutists when they finally attacked occupied France on D-Day, 6th June 1944.

## A BUSY LIFE

Unlike soldiers who often had to wait in their bases for something to happen, the 600,000 men of the RAF were always busy. All the jobs on an airbase required a

high degree of technical skill so a lot of time was spent in training.

There was work for aircrew in all areas of the war and there was always some job for them to do. Despite the hard work and the danger of a job where often the only chance of survival was a parachute, there were always plenty of volunteers to serve in the Royal Air Force.

## WAAF

The *Women's Auxiliary Air Force* (WAAF), like the Wrens, were not allowed to be involved in the fighting but did many of the men's jobs so that they could be free to fight. Some women were pilots on planes that transported urgent supplies and others mapped the positions of friendly

| 18th January 1943 | 31st January 1943 | 9th February 1943 |
|---|---|---|
| The Russian Army breaks through to the city of Leningrad, which has been under siege from the German Army for sixteen months. | Despite strict orders from Hitler not to, the German troops at the battle of Stalingrad surrender. The German soldiers are starving, cold and have little ammunition left with which to fight. | After a six month battle for the control of Guadalcanal in the Solomon Islands, the American forces have won and the Japanese have withdrawn. |

and enemy aircraft at Bomber Command Headquarters. Other Waafs staffed airforce canteens and offices and some had the very heavy job of setting up and

In Remembrance of Squadron Leader Alan Sudbury Cussens, an Old Boy of this School, who gave his life for his country as Pilot of a Mosquito aircraft, over Brest 1st December, 1943.
Presented to

THE ALAN CUSSENS MEMORIAL.

maintaining barrage balloon stations. At first it was thought that the job of moving the barrage balloons into position would be too strenuous for a woman. However the Waafs managed the job and became so skilled that less women were needed to do the job than was originally planned.

# THINGS TO DO

**1** *Make a parachute:* You will need: a piece of material about 25 cms square (kitchen towel will work); four pieces of thin string or wool about 30 cms in length; a weight of some sort (a stone; a rubber; a lump of plasticine).

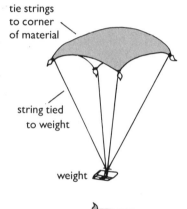

tie strings to corner of material

string tied to weight

weight

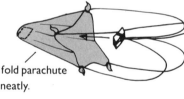

fold parachute neatly.

To make your parachute work you can either throw it high in the air or, taking great care, throw it out of an upstairs window. Either way it should open and fall to the ground like a real parachute.

**2** Draw an aerial picture of your area – show houses, schools, factories, shops, fields etc. and try to colour it the way things would appear from the air – so you would use the roof colour and not the colour of the walls.

**3** Aircrew were often given maps printed on silk. This was so that the map would fold up very small and could be easily hidden.

Try to make your own material map using a spare piece of plain cloth. You can use felt tips to draw a map of your local area on the material but special fabric pens or crayons will make sure that the map will not "run" if it gets wet.

| 16th February 1943 | 10th March 1943 | 15th April 1943 |
|---|---|---|
| The Russians are winning many battles against the Germans. In the last ten days they have recaptured four Russian towns including the town of Kharkov. | Since the beginning of the month the RAF have been bombing the Ruhr valley, the major industrial area in Germany. Much damage has been done but the Germans insist war production is not affected. | The RAF drop huge bombs of 8,000 lbs (nicknamed the "Blockbuster") and 4,000 lbs (nicknamed the "Factory-Smasher") on the German town of Stuttgart. |

# SOLDIERS

When men in any country were *conscripted* they would most likely be sent into the Army. In June 1941 there were two and a quarter million men in the British Army but only a small proportion of them were involved in any fighting. Large numbers of soldiers were stationed in army camps throughout Britain, waiting for something to happen.

## WAITING TIME

In the retreat from Dunkirk the Army had left a huge amount of weapons and equipment in France ranging from rifles and tin hats to tanks and large artillery guns. The loss of this equipment plus the fact that Hitler had time to turn Europe into a "fortress", meant that Britain had no chance of retaking Europe. It was not until the American Army's soldiers (GIs) added strength of numbers to the Allies, that an attack on mainland Europe could be considered. Meanwhile for thousands of British soldiers there was little fighting to be done.

The attempt to fight off Hitler's Blitzkreig in Europe had shown how a well-trained army like that of Germany, even with less men and equipment, could defeat a poorly trained one. After Dunkirk much of the British soldiers' time was taken up in training for the fighting.

There was also a feeling among the government and generals, such as "Monty" Montgomery, that a better educated and informed army would be more effective. So formal education became part of army training. The army set up the *ABCA* (Army Bureau of Current Affairs) which organized lectures and discussions so that the ordinary soldier could feel involved and knowledgeable about who and why he was fighting, rather than just following orders.

Soldiers, not needed to fight in the various areas of the world where battles were taking place, were very useful in helping to fight fires and repair bomb damage during and after air raids.

## NICKNAMES

American soldiers were known as "GIs". This name came from the initials of General Issue which was the term used to describe the uniform and kit the men were given.

Soldiers from Australia and New Zealand were known as "ANZACS" from the initial letters of Australian and New Zealand Army Corps.

"TOMMIES" was the nickname for British soldiers. This came from the name Thomas Atkinson which was used by the British Army as a sample name to show soldiers how to fill in forms.

## THE FIGHTING

Long range rifles and guns, grenades and tanks made it possible to kill an enemy

---

**20th April 1943**

The church bells of Britain can be rung normally again. The ringing of church bells was banned in June 1940 unless it was to warn of an invasion.

**12th May 1943**

German and Italian troops surrender in North Africa and the fighting there stops. 110,000 Germans and 40,000 Italians are taken prisoner.

**17th May 1943**

The Mohne and Eder Dams on the River Ruhr are breached by specially designed "bouncing bombs" dropped by RAF bombers. The flood of water released causes great damage.

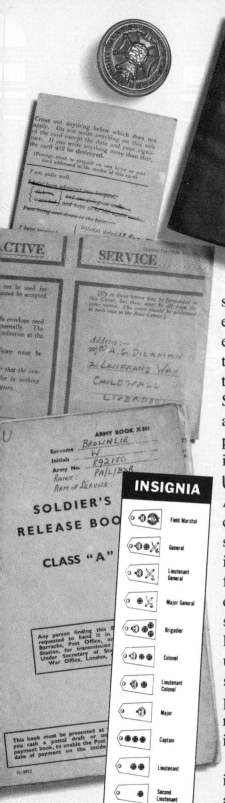

the fields and woods of Europe but in the desert German soldiers' uniforms became more like the khaki colour of British uniforms. In Far Eastern jungles soldiers' tin helmets were covered in a netting which allowed sticks and leaves to be added to the hat as camouflage.

## AREAS OF FIGHTING

After Dunkirk, the main area of fighting in which British soldiers were involved was in North Africa against the Italian and German armies. But towards the end of the war, British soldiers were to be found fighting throughout the world in many different sorts of battlefield.

- In the fighting in North Africa there was little defensive terrain, like woods and hills, so the campaign moved quickly and tanks played the major role on both sides.
- When the Allies invaded Sicily and the Italian mainland, the German and Italian armies made use of good defensive terrain and the Allied advance was slow.
- Some of the fiercest fighting took place against the Japanese in the jungles of Burma and Malaya, and the islands of the Pacific Ocean.

soldier from a distance. In earlier wars, even to some extent in the First World War, there was a great deal of hand to hand fighting but in the Second World War the weapons and equipment an army possessed became very important.

## UNIFORMS

As the war went on, uniforms changed to become most suitable for the circumstances in which the soldiers were fighting. For example, in the desert, the standard British soldier's uniform was ludicrously hot. Everyday uniform became shorts, short-sleeved shirts and hats which protected the soldier's head, rather than the tin helmets worn in colder climates.

Camouflage dress was very important. The grey of German army uniforms worked well in

### INSIGNIA

| | |
|---|---|
| | Field Marshal |
| | General |
| | Lieutenant General |
| | Major General |
| | Brigadier |
| | Colonel |
| | Lieutenant Colonel |
| | Major |
| | Captain |
| | Lieutenant |
| | Second Lieutenant |

| 12th June 1943 | 10th July 1943 | 19th July 1943 |
|---|---|---|
| The Italian islands of Pantelleria and Lampedusa have been taken by the Allies. | The Allies invade the major Italian island of Sicily. | Hitler and Mussolini meet in Northern Italy to discuss the Allies' successes in attacking Italy. Meanwhile US planes bomb factories, airfields and railyards in Rome. |

- The longest and most bloody series of battles took place on the *Eastern Front* between the German Army and the huge but poorly-equipped Russian Red Army.

## ATS

The women's branch of the army was called the *Auxiliary Territorial Services* (ATS). There were more women, about 198,000, in the ATS than in the Wrens (74,000) or in the Waafs (171,000). As with the other women's services the ATS were not to be involved in the fighting but large numbers of ATS women staffed the anti-aircraft guns. Some ATS women had the very dangerous job of controlling the searchlights that swept the sky for enemy aircraft.

Many ATS women had jobs as drivers. After a short course in mechanics they were given a vehicle, anything from a motorbike to a lorry. From then on they were supposed to be responsible for the vehicle, driving it and carrying out all maintenance on it.

The ATS also staffed the mobile kitchens that fed the fighting soldiers on bases all over the world, as well as offering food and comfort to civilians during and after air raids.

**SAFE CONDUCT**

*The soldier who carries this safe conduct is using it as a sign of his genuine wish to give himself up. He is to be disarmed, to be well looked after, to receive food and medical attention as required, and to* from the danger zone as soon as possible.

H.R. Alexander
FIELD MARSHAL
Supreme Allied Commander in the Mediterranean Theatre of Operations

## CONSCIENTIOUS OBJECTORS

Some men and women believed that it was wrong to fight and would not join the armed forces. They were called conscientious objectors. If they could prove that their beliefs were strongly held they were given the choice of work that did not involve fighting. For example many became involved with A.R.P. work or were members of ambulance teams. Others worked in coal mines or in the bomb disposal units.

When the D-Day invasion of Europe began many conscientious objectors – as members of the Parachute Field Ambulance – were among the first to land in France. They carried no weapons and were there only to help the wounded.

## THINGS TO DO

**1** Make a large picture of a World War Two soldier. You can either paint it or make it a collage or use paint and collage together. Choose the army and try to make the uniform as accurate as possible.

**2** Interview someone who was in the forces during the Second World War. Make a list of questions to ask them and try to record your interview on audio or video cassette.

| 25th July 1943 | 3rd August 1943 | 17th August 1943 |
|---|---|---|
| Mussolini resigns as leader of Italy. He is replaced by his political opponent, Marshall Badoglio. | Continuing the Allied attack on German industries, the port of Hamburg has been bombed by the RAF at night and the US airforce by day for more than a week. 10,000 tons of bombs have been dropped. | Despite Mussolini's resignation the Italians have not yet surrendered, but the Allies now have control of Sicily. |

# WORK

War creates a lot of extra work. As well as needing people to do the fighting, there is also huge demand for weapons. In Britain nearly three and a half million men were in the armed forces and those men had left jobs behind. Something had to be done to replace them. Before the war a woman generally stopped work once she married and spent her time as a housewife whether or not she had children. All this changed with the Second World War.

## RESERVED OCCUPATIONS
Some men could not be spared to go into the armed forces. These men worked in *Reserved Occupations* as their experience and training meant that it would be difficult to replace them − farmers, train drivers, policemen, some civil servants and other workers were thought to be of more use keeping the country running smoothly than joining the fighting. At the beginning of the war this did not mean that these men could not volunteer to join the armed forces and in some jobs so many men "joined up" that certain work came under

an *Essential Work Order* (EWO). An EWO meant that a worker could not be sacked or leave their job, even if they wanted to. This was to make sure there were always enough workers in each type of job.

## CONSCRIPTION
*Conscription* is a system by which the government registers people and then tells them what job they have to do. At first conscription only applied to men between the ages of 18 and 41. Most of them were sent to the army, navy or the airforce, although some of them would have volunteered to join the armed forces before the government "called them up".

In December 1941 Britain became the first country ever to conscript women. It started with unmarried women between the ages of 20 and 30 but by July 1943 all women not looking after children under 14 as well as men aged 18-51, had to be registered and made to do some sort of war work. Women were given the choice of working in a weapons' factory, in the women's services or on the land.

TAKING OVER? GOOD FOR YOU! WE'LL SHOW HITLER!

THOUSANDS OF WOMEN
AGED 17½−50 WANTED
TO BECOME COOKS
IN THE ATS AND WAAF

## FACTORIES
Most factories had to change or adapt the products they made. Some factories like Cadburys Chocolate and Yardley Cosmetics continued production but turned over most of their factory to making war products such as shell

---

| 8th September 1943 | 12th September 1943 | 25th September 1943 |
|---|---|---|
| Italy makes an unconditional surrender to the Allies, following their invasion of the Italian mainland five days previously. | German soldiers rescue Mussolini from imprisonment in Italy. Although the Italians have surrendered, a large force of German troops continue to fight the Allies on Italian soil. | The Russian Army continues to make great advances against the Germans, recapturing much of the Russian territory taken in the Blitzkrieg of 1941. Today the Red Army took back Smolensk. |

cases or small parts for aircraft.

Other factories, called *Royal Ordnance Factories,* were built by the government. These did most of the work involving the handling of explosives. Some of the factories made the explosives and others put these explosives into bombs, shells, mines and grenades. Because of the danger of explosion, these factories were often situated a few miles out of town and the workers had long and difficult journeys to reach them.

Factory work was often boring and repetitive but the lives of soldiers, sailors and airmen depended upon the quality of work the factories produced. Conditions inside the factories were often not very pleasant. The Blackout windows made the inside stuffy and allowed no daylight through. Another problem was that many of the factories had only ever been staffed by men so that there were no proper facilities, like toilets and rest rooms, for women. Conditions did improve during the war as the government and employers realized that the happier people were, the better the job they did.

## LONG HOURS

The normal working hours were 8½ hours a day, Monday to Friday and 4 hours on a Saturday morning, but most workers usually worked at least a 10 hour day because they were required to do overtime.

For women especially, these long hours created many problems. Most women still did the family shopping and they had to shop where they were registered. Shops were usually open from 9-6 p.m. so the only time that the factory worker could shop was on her Saturday afternoon off. With very little free-time and no washing machines, dishwashers or vacuum cleaners, keeping the house clean and tidy was almost impossible.

Some women had to work despite the fact they had young children. If a woman's husband was away in the forces money would be short and she might have to work. Getting someone to look after the children was difficult until the government began to open nurseries where children could stay all day while their mothers worked.

## WAGES

During the war women were employed on jobs which had only been done by men before. These jobs included ship-building; welding; unloading cargo ships; making steel; building tanks and planes. Yet women were not paid the same wages as the men who did the jobs before or even the men working alongside them. Generally women were paid about half the amount men were paid. In 1943 a survey found that while men's average weekly wages were £6.1s.4d. (£6.06), women's average wages were only £3.2s.11d. (£3.15). Many women tried hard for better pay but even the trade unions did not give them much support and women's wages were one area which showed no improvement during the war.

SPEED THE PLOUGH!
WIN OUR GREAT PRODUCTION FIGHT

Farmers! Look at Spring with Winter in your mind—next winter, when feeding stuffs will be short unless you grow your own.

Every acre you plough now means more fodder to carry you through next winter.

★THE PRIME MINISTER TO FARMERS AND WORKERS—

PLOUGH NOW!

| 4th October 1943 | 13th October 1943 | 2nd December 1943 |
|---|---|---|
| The French island of Corsica is liberated by the French Resistance as the occupying German forces are defeated. | Italy declares war on Germany as fierce fighting continues between German and Allied soldiers in Italy. | One in ten conscripted men will have to work in the coal mines instead of joining the forces. These men are being called "Bevin Boys" after Ernest Bevin, the Minister of Labour, who introduced the scheme. |

42

# BEVIN BOYS

Coal mining was a particularly hard, dirty and underpaid job. Although it was a reserved occupation many miners preferred to join the forces than stay in mining. Women were not allowed to become coal miners and the government could never get enough men to work in the mines.

In December 1943 a way was devised to have enough workers for the mines. When men were conscripted a ballot was taken and one man in every ten had to go into the mines rather than join the armed forces. It was a system hated by the conscripts, most of whom would rather have risked the fighting than work in a mine. As most of the men were only 18 and the Minister responsible for this plan was called Ernest Bevin, these mine workers became known as *Bevin Boys*.

# PART - TIME AND OUTWORK

Nearly all part-time workers were women who could only spare half a day to work, usually because they had children to look after. These women worked because they wanted to help the war effort.

Together with many disabled and elderly people, these women became *outworkers*, doing such jobs as making and assembling small machine parts at home.

Everyone wanted to help the war effort. Teachers and older school pupils would spend their school holidays working in factories and people who had office jobs during the week often worked on Sundays in factories so that factory workers could have a day off.

## WORK ON THE LAND

It was vital that Britain grew more of her own food to save on imports which risked sailors' lives. Many farm workers had either joined the armed forces or gone to work in the much better paid factory jobs. Without the workers to farm the land, producing enough food would have been impossible.

Children helped during the school holidays and many factory workers spent nearly all of their weekends helping on farms. Everywhere were posters and adverts asking people to *Lend a Hand on the Land* or to take a holiday on a farm where they would be expected to help with the farm work. For many people from bombed cities a holiday on a farm, even with work, was something to be enjoyed.

Some other people who worked on the farms had less choice about being there. Italian and German prisoners-of-war were often used for farm work but the *Women's Land Army* was by far the most important source of farm labour during the war.

## WOMEN'S LAND ARMY

The Women's Land Army, or Land Girls as they became known, had a uniform but it was not really like being in the Army. Women would live on the farm where they worked or in a hostel with other Land Girls. They would spend all

---

| 26th December 1943 | 22nd January 1944 | 28th January 1944 |
|---|---|---|
| The German Navy has lost one of her major warships. The *Scharnhorst* was sunk by the Royal Navy after it had attacked an Allied convoy on its way to Russia. | In Italy the Allies make a surprise landing from the sea at Anzio. This attack is behind the German lines and is an attempt to defeat the Germans in Italy. | Reports of Japanese cruelty and ill treatment of Allied prisoners-of-war are announced in the House of Commons. |

day, sometimes as many as fourteen hours, working. Their work included milking, ploughing, tree-felling, rat catching and any other of the many jobs on a farm. Many of the Women's Land Army were town girls of eighteen or nineteen with no experience of country or farm life but by the end of the war no farmer would have wanted to be without them.

**2** Find out if any factories near you were working during the war. What did they make in wartime and what do they make now?

Most factories presented their workers with a certificate at the end of the war to thank them for their hard work. Design your own certificate. You could use the name of a real factory or make up your own.

**3** Try some of these "growing" projects:

(a) Buy a packet of mustard and cress seeds. Moisten some kitchen paper and put it in the bottom of a margarine tub. Sprinkle the seeds over the paper. Keep the paper moist and on a sunny window sill and within a few days you will have cress ready to eat.

(b) Grow your own radishes from seed. They will be ready to eat in about six weeks' time. You can grow them in a window box or deep seed tray, as long as you have at least 10 cms of soil. Follow the instructions on the seed packet carefully.

(c) If you are lucky enough to have a patch of garden for yourself try planting some vegetables like carrots, parsnips or runner beans. Follow the instructions on the seed packet and keep a diary of when and what you plant, how it grows and how much you harvest.

## THINGS TO DO

**1** WORD SEARCH
Find the following jobs in the grid. They were all jobs which were either reserved occupations or had an Essential Work Order placed on them. One of the jobs has been split into two.

DRAUGHTSMAN  FARMER
VET DOCKER  BUS DRIVER
MERCHANT SEAMAN
TRAIN DRIVER  BAKER
COALMINER  PHYSICIST
CIVIL SERVANT  FIREMAN
POLICEMAN  ENGINEER
LIGHTHOUSE KEEPER

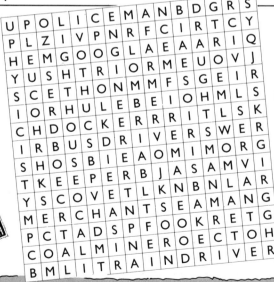

| U | P | O | L | I | C | E | M | A | N | B | D | G | R | S |
| P | L | Z | I | V | P | N | R | F | C | I | R | T | C | Y |
| H | E | M | G | O | O | G | L | A | E | A | A | R | I | Q |
| Y | U | S | H | T | R | I | O | R | M | E | U | O | V | J |
| S | C | E | T | H | O | N | M | M | F | S | G | E | I | R |
| I | O | R | H | U | L | E | B | E | I | O | H | M | L | S |
| C | H | D | O | C | K | E | R | R | R | I | T | L | S | K |
| I | R | B | U | S | D | R | I | V | E | R | S | W | E | R |
| S | H | O | S | B | I | E | A | O | M | I | M | O | R | G |
| T | K | E | E | P | E | R | B | J | A | S | A | M | V | I |
| Y | S | C | O | V | E | T | L | K | N | B | N | L | A | R |
| M | E | R | C | H | A | N | T | S | E | A | M | A | N | G |
| P | C | T | A | D | S | P | F | O | O | K | R | E | T | G |
| C | O | A | L | M | I | N | E | R | O | E | C | T | O | H |
| B | M | L | I | T | R | A | I | N | D | R | I | V | E | R |

**29th February 1944**
American troops today went ashore at Los Negros in the Admiralty islands. The Allies are having much success in the Pacific Area and captured the Marshall Islands earlier this month.

**19th March 1944**
Using gliders the Allies land a large, self-contained force of men in Japanese occupied Burma. Within 12 hours of the landing the Allied forces have constructed a large air strip in the jungle.

**1st April 1944**
All visitors are banned from going within ten miles of the south coast of England. This is to give the forces room to practise for the D-Day landings.

# NEWS & INFORMATION

**Sunday Pictorial**

March 4, 1945
No. 1,564
TWOPENCE

# BATTLE FOR THE RHINE HAS BECOME A CHASE

This Is a German Family, Homeless They Flee, for Now It Is— **Their Turn**

WITH yesterday's link-up of two great armies under Field-Marshal Montgomery, the Canadian First and the American Ninth, the whole battle for the West Rhineland last night became a chase.

A quarter of a million Allied troops, American, British and Canadian, raced to the Rhine, tearing into the battered remnants of the pride of Rundstedt's forces.

Small suicide squads of do-or-die Nazis were left behind in villages and farms in a desperate attempt to provide cover for twenty thousand fleeing Nazis.

Cooks, bakers and convalescent troops were flung by the Nazis into these frantic rearguard fights.

From north, south and east the steel claws of the Allies was closing in on the Germans. Great fires burned like beacons of doom on the west bank of the Rhine as the stricken Nazis struggled to get back across to the other bank.

called Dr Goebbels, was to convince the Germans that they were superior to everyone else. "The Germans are a super-race destined to rule the world" was one propaganda slogan often repeated.

In Britain most people were determined not to believe bad things about the Germans. Propaganda during the First World War had convinced the British people that the Germans, or "Huns" as they were called, were a wicked nation. When they discovered that the German people were really just the same as them, they were ashamed and in the Second World War the

*Issued by the Ministry of Information in co-operation with the War Office and the Ministry of Home Security*

## Beating the INVADER

In Britain during the Second World War there were three ways to get news. One was from cinema newsreels; another was from BBC Radio and the third was from the daily newspapers. All news was *censored,* that is checked by the government to prevent the enemy gaining information such as the number of soldiers in the army; the sites of factories or airbases or where the navy's warships were going. The government did not tell news reporters what to write but they did tell them what they could not write. If the government wanted to put

out their own information, they used the Ministry of Information.

### PROPAGANDA

Information put out by a government to persuade people to do or to believe what the government wants is called *propaganda.* Both sides in the war used propaganda for many different purposes.

In Germany especially, most propaganda, put out by a Nazi

government knew that the same sort of propaganda would not work. Instead it had to concentrate on propaganda which made people work together and believe in what they were fighting for.

The cinema played a part in this sort of gentle propaganda. Films and documentaries were made showing glamorous and attractive young men and women in factories, army camps, airbases or on ships at

| 25th May 1944 | 26th May 1944 | 4th June 1944 |
|---|---|---|
| The main German line of defence in Italy is broken by the Allies. German troops are now retreating. | The Allies bomb several French cities in preparation for the D-Day landing, the place and date for which is still a secret. | Rome, the capital of Italy, is "liberated" by the Allies. Most Italians are delighted and glad to see the Germans go. |

sea. These sort of films suggested the value in working together to save the British way of life which was under threat from Hitler.

## PROPAGANDA FROM THE SKIES
Both Allies and Axis powers used planes to drop propaganda leaflets to people on the ground. Just before Dunkirk, the Germans dropped leaflets shaped like leaves into France. They were printed with "If you fight England's battles your soldiers will fall like autumn leaves."

The Allies used to drop leaflets to German and Italian soldiers which they said would guarantee them safe passage if they surrendered.

## CAMPAIGNS
There was a great deal of other information which the government needed to pass on to people, and some of this could be called propaganda. The Ministry of Information had its own film unit which made short information films but the vast majority of information was given in poster, advertisement and leaflet campaigns. Throughout the war there were a huge number of campaigns. Here is a sample of some :

Always carry your gas mask
Women – join the factories
Help fight with the firebomb fighters
Keep your children safe in the country
How to behave in an air raid shelter
Do not waste food
Take care in the Blackout
Dig for Victory
Join the Home Guard
Careless Talk Costs Lives

"........ but for Heaven's sake don't say I told you!"

CARELESS TALK COSTS LIVES

MUSEUM OF LONDON

## CARELESS TALK COSTS LIVES
The "Dig for Victory" and "Careless Talk Costs Lives" campaigns were probably the most effective and best remembered. In the "Careless Talk Costs Lives" campaign the government's aim was to persuade people that any conversation about the war could put men's lives in danger. It showed how even two women talking on the bus about their soldier sons could give vital information to any enemy spy who happened to be listening. Many posters showed cartoon drawings of two people chatting about the war with Hitler under a table – or hidden elsewhere – listening to every word.

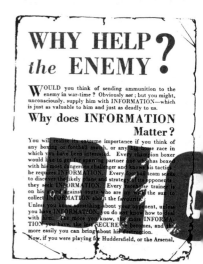

WHY HELP ?
the ENEMY ?

WOULD you think of sending ammunition to the enemy in war-time ? Obviously *not* ; but you might, unconsciously, supply him with INFORMATION—which is just as valuable to him and just as deadly to us.

**Why does INFORMATION Matter ?**

You will realise the extreme importance if you think of any boxing or football match, or any horse race in which you have been interested. Every champion boxer would like to get for sparring partner one who has boxed with his most dangerous challenger and knows his tactics; he requires INFORMATION. Every football team seeks to discover the likely plans and strategy of its opponents; they seek INFORMATION. Every racehorse trainer is on his guard against touts who are out with the sun to collect INFORMATION about the favourite.

Unless you know something about your opponent, unless you have INFORMATION, you do not know how to deal with him. The more you know, the more INFORMATION you have, the less SECURE he becomes, and the more easily you can bring about his destruction.

Now, if you were playing for Huddersfield, or the Arsenal,

| 6th June 1944 | 15th June 1944 | 22nd June 1944 |
|---|---|---|
| D-Day Landings. This is the beginning of a major attack in Normandy and invasion of the European mainland. | For the first time planes taking off from land bases in the U.S.A. have been able to reach Japan. Boeing B29 Superfortresses have bombed the Japanese mainland. | The Allies capture two VI launch sites in the Cherbourg Peninsula in France. It is only nine days since the first VI landed in Britain – but the Germans have other launch sites. |

## BBC RADIO NEWS

Cinema newsreels provided a round up of what had happened in the previous few days or weeks. But for up-to-date news the people relied on radio and the daily newspapers.

In July 1940 BBC news-readers began to introduce themselves. Before the war their names were never announced. It was felt that if people got to know the news-readers, any attempt by Hitler to broadcast in place of the BBC would be spotted at once. As well as news bulletins for Britain, the BBC World Service broadcast every day in twenty three languages, including German, into occupied Europe. The information given was as accurate as possible and for many people in the occupied countries it kept them in touch with the Allies. Even German people listened to the BBC as they felt it gave them a fairly true picture of how the war was going. It was, however, against the law and anyone in Europe who did listen to the BBC did so in secret.

## OR VICTORY NOW!

## LORD HAW HAW

While the BBC World Service was trying to encourage the forces and Resistance abroad, the Germans were broadcasting programmes into Britain. The most famous broadcaster working for the Nazis was a man called William Joyce who became known as Lord Haw Haw. He told many stories of how good life was in Germany compared to Britain but his propaganda failed to work and most people only laughed at him.

## NEWSPAPERS

Newspaper editors faced many difficulties trying to produce a paper every day during the war. The censor stopped them writing about certain things and often blacked out large sections of photographs in case the enemy could gain information from them. The shortage of paper meant that most of the time papers were only four or six pages long and despite a big demand for daily papers, only limited numbers could be printed each day.

Journalists, too, were in short supply, as were press photographers, as many were called up into the forces. Those journalists left were free to make comments about the news and most newspapers supported the government on most issues. The *Daily Mirror* was felt by some government ministers to be too critical of the government's handling of the war but the majority of people respected the paper as reporting and commenting fairly and accurately.

## THINGS TO DO

**1** Imagine you are a reporter and you have to give a report on the RAF's 1000 bomber raid on Cologne. You can choose either to:
(a) Write a newspaper report.
(b) Write a script for a BBC radio news report and record it if you can.
(c) Write the script for a cinema newsreel. Imagine you have some film of the planes leaving their air base; of Cologne on fire, and the planes returning home.

**2** Design an advert for a newspaper reminding people that "Careless Talk Costs Lives." Remember you can only use black and white.

| 3rd July 1944 | 20th July 1944 | 31st July 1944 |
|---|---|---|
| Children are being evacuated from London and other parts of the South East that are in the path of the VI rocket bombs or doodlebugs as they are sometimes called. | A bomb explodes in Hitler's H.Q. in an attempt to kill him. The attempt is thought to have been made in a plot by some of his own Generals. | The Allies have control of Normandy. Fierce fighting has brought a great deal of destruction to much of Normandy. |

# ENTERTAINMENT

There was no television whatsoever throughout the war. The BBC Television service was closed down on 1st September 1939 but at that time it had only been operating for three years and very few people had television sets. People were much more affected by the closure of cinemas, theatres and dance halls but fortunately most of these were open again by December 1939.

Early on in the war, people spent more time at home as visiting friends and relatives was made difficult, not least because of the Blackout. There was also a shortage of petrol which not only affected those lucky enough to have a car but also meant that public transport was not as reliable. At home, people occupied themselves reading, sewing, listening to the radio, or doing household repairs. However, as the war went on, entertainment became increasingly important. Life had become difficult with longer working hours and only limited amounts of food and clothes and no luxuries at all.

Entertainment therefore helped to take people's minds off the hardship and dullness of wartime life.

## RADIO PROGRAMMES

The BBC was the only broadcasting company in Britain and with the outbreak of war they cut their radio stations to only one. All through the war this was the only official channel, although there were also propaganda programmes broadcast from Germany (see News and Information Section page 47).
The BBC were proud of the fact that during the war they never once had to stop transmitting their programmes despite all the bombing. If one transmitter was damaged they would switch to another in a different part of the country.

BBC radio provided hours of happy listening and many programmes introduced during the war remained as favourites for several years afterwards.
● The most popular programme during the war was a comedy called *ITMA* (It's That Man Again). This starred

a man called Tommy Handley who broadcast sketches which made fun of everyone involved in the war. The programme had a number of characters like "Funf", the useless German Spy; "Mrs Mopp the Corporation Cleanser" and "His Washout the Mayor of Foaming in the Mouth" who did and said ridiculous things.
● Another very popular programme was *The Brains Trust* which was based on questions sent in to the BBC by listeners. Questions ranged from "How does a fly land on the ceiling?" to more serious subjects. The questions were read out on the programme to a panel of "brains", experts in different subjects who would discuss the various points.
● Other programmes offered advice on all sorts of subjects. *The Radio Doctor* advised on health matters and *Woman's Hour* and other similar programmes gave advice on how to make rations go further and how to "make do and mend".
● The BBC also broadcast a number of serious plays

| 8th August 1944 | 12th August 1944 | 25th August 1944 |
|---|---|---|
| After a brief trial, several high-ranking officers in Hitler's Army are executed for their part in the bomb plot which attempted to kill Hitler last month. | Running from the Isle of Wight to Northern France, the first PLUTO (Pipe Line Under The Ocean) begins to send fuel to the Allied forces. | To the delight of most French people, Paris has been taken by the Allies. The swastika on the Eiffel Tower has been replaced by the French flag. |

like Shakespeare's *Hamlet*.

● A great favourite with children was a programme called *Children's Hour* which was presented by a man known as "Uncle Mac". *Children's Hour* included stories, songs and sketches with characters like *Larry the Lamb* and *Dennis the Dachshund*.

● Music programmes of all sorts were very popular. Request programmes were a new idea and soon built up large audiences, for example *Forces Favourites,* where people wrote in and asked for something to be played for a friend or relative serving abroad.

● Radio programmes were enormously popular in factories, too, and programmes

## ENSA

ENSA (Entertainments National Service Association) spent all its time entertaining people in army, airforce and naval bases, as well as in factories. Comedians, bands of musicians and singers, sometimes famous ones like Vera Lynne, George Formby and Gracie Fields would give concerts or dances in factory canteens at lunchtime or after work. Putting on film shows and plays was another part of ENSA's work and often the concerts and shows were performed at locations only a few miles from the fighting.

like *Music While You Work* were broadcast to cheer up the factory workers on the production line. Eventually the BBC began making some broadcasts from inside factories, army, airforce and naval bases and these also proved very popular.

## CINEMA

The cinema was always very popular with both adults and children. Nearly everyone went at least once a week and as many cinemas changed their main film during the week, it was possible to see two or three big films in one week at the same cinema. The majority of the films came from America's Hollywood, although a few British films were still made. Charlie Chaplin's *The Great Dictator,* a film which made fun of Hitler, was popular but generally people did not want to watch films that reminded them of the war. Musical films and romantic films like *Gone with the Wind* were in great demand as they helped people forget about the war for a short time.

Children had special cinema shows on a Saturday morning. There would be short films and cartoons and always a serial such as *Tarzan, The Lone Ranger* or *Flash Gordon*. At the

MUSEUM OF LONDON

| 27th August 1944 | 9th September 1944 | 15th September 1944 |
|---|---|---|
| The Russians have uncovered the first of the Nazi death camps to be found by the Allies. It is thought that 1½ million people have been murdered at the Maidenek Concentration Camp. | The first V2 rocket bomb lands on London. More powerful than the V1s the shock wave when they land can be felt for miles. | The Allies have broken through the heavily defended German border known as the "Siegfried Line". Belgium was liberated ten days ago and German troops are in retreat throughout occupied Europe. |

end of each episode the hero would be left in such trouble that everyone in the cinema would want to go back the next week to see what happened.

## READING

Magazines and books were another popular form of entertainment. The *Dandy* and *Beano* comics were printed throughout the war, as well as women's magazines like *Good Housekeeping*. Magazines of short stories and poems also sold well, especially to soldiers who spent a great deal of time waiting for the next battle with nothing much to do. Soldiers were also desperate for books to read. Large numbers of old books were pulped to provide new paper and although new books were published there were far fewer printed than before the war. So books were always in short supply and the few that were available were read keenly by lots of people.

## SPORT

Football was by far the most popular spectator sport in 1939. When the war started the leagues were reorganized into areas to prevent clubs having to travel long distances for games. Football clubs, like all other sports, lost large numbers of their players to the armed forces. Often teenage boys were all that was left to make up the teams, but clubs were allowed to play guest players. So if a former professional footballer was not required by his army, navy or airforce unit, he could play the occasional game for any club he chose.

Crowds at football grounds were cut on orders from the government, in case a ground was bombed. In fact, although grounds were damaged by bombs, no one was ever killed or injured at a match and so by the 1943 season, football was almost as well attended as before the war.

| 17th September 1944 | 14th October 1944 | 20th October 1944 |
|---|---|---|
| The "blackout" in Britain ends and the "dim-out" begins. Some street lighting is allowed and railway stations, buses and trains will have adequate lighting again. | The Allies liberate Athens, the capital city of Greece. The streets are filled with cheering crowds. | Aachen is the first German town to fall into Allied hands. So far this month the Allies have liberated much of Greece and Belgrade in Yugoslavia. |

Just as some sports grounds suffered bomb damage, others were used for the war effort. Twickenham, the home of English rugby union, was made into allotments for people to grow their own food. The Oval cricket ground at Kennington in London became a prisoner-of-war camp and many other sports grounds, including Epsom Race Course, were taken over by the military.

Horse and greyhound racing continued all through the war with races arranged so that the animals and people involved did not have to travel far. Rugby and cricket continued in much the same way as football, making up any team possible. This meant that sometimes spectators would see a very high quality game played between large numbers of internationals while other matches might have no first class players at all.

## CHILDREN'S GAMES

The war made some differences to children's play. The Blackout meant that it was difficult to play out either in the dark or early evening. Indoor games like cards, Ludo, Monopoly and Tiddly Winks became very important to children, especially in winter.

When playing outside, children still played most of the same games they had before the war. "Pretend" games of mums and dads, hospitals and especially soldiers and pilots were all popular. There were skipping games, chasing games, ball games and marbles. There were also wooden "tops" which were "whipped" to make them spin and hoops which were rolled along with the help of a stick.

The war provided children with a new game to play outside: collecting war souvenirs. Children, especially in towns, would play among the ruined buildings of a bomb site and many made collections of bits of bombs, crashed planes, and anything else they could lay their hands on. These were not perhaps the safest of games and were discouraged by adults, but the children loved them.

## THINGS TO DO

**1** Design a film poster for a film called *Strike up the Band.* This was a musical film from 1940 that starred Judy Garland and Mickey Rooney as members of a high school band that took part in a radio contest to find the best band.

**2** Find out what happened to your local football team and its ground during the war.

**3** Interview someone who was a child during the war. Make a list of questions to ask them about their life then. Try to tape the interview on audio or video cassette.

Listen to your three taped interviews from the Rationing, Soldiers and this section. As you listen try to pick out in what ways life was similar for all three people and in what ways it was different.

| 21st October 1944 | 11th November 1944 | 12th November 1944 |
|---|---|---|
| The Americans have landed in Leyte, one of the main Philippine Islands. The sea battle which took place offshore has virtually destroyed the Japanese Navy. | The Home Guard is disbanded – although the members are allowed to keep their uniforms and weapons. | The last of Germany's warships, the *Tirpitz*, has been destroyed by RAF bombers which dropped special armour piercing bombs on the ship. This means the German Navy can no longer threaten shipping. |

# RESISTANCE

## FORTRESS EUROPE

After Britain had retreated from Dunkirk in the summer of 1940 the German Army continued its advance, and by the summer of 1942 nearly every country in Europe had surrendered to Hitler. Norway never officially surrendered but there, as everywhere else, the armies stopped fighting. Britain could only fight Germany through air raids, battles in North Africa and at sea. Europe was left under the control of the German Army. It was defended like a fortress and Britain and the Allies did not have the strength, until the summer of 1944, to attack Hitler's "Fortress Europe". It was left to the ordinary people in the occupied countries of Europe to organize resistance movements and fight against Nazi rule.

## LIFE UNDER THE NAZIS

The Nazis ruled the countries they occupied by fear and terror. Hitler had a secret police force, called the *Gestapo,* who watched over the people and made sure they obeyed the strict laws. The laws were to try to control the people and did not allow them out of their homes at certain times; forbade them to listen to certain radio broadcasts such as the BBC and did not allow them to read certain books and newspapers. There were many other regulations too, and punishments for breaking the law were very severe.

Any action against the occupying Germans was punished very severely indeed. For example, Hitler ordered a terrible revenge after the death of a man called Heydrich, who ruled an area of Czechoslovakia. The Gestapo went to a small village called Lidice, just outside Prague, Czechoslovakia's capital city. There they took all the 199 men and boys from the village and shot them. The 195 women of the village were sent to one concentration camp and the 90 village children to another. Then the Gestapo knocked down every building in the village and ploughed the rubble into the soil.

In all the occupied countries the Nazis regarded people as little more than slaves to provide labour for Germany. The occupied countries were seen as land to provide food for the German people. The Nazis did not care if the occupied peoples were starving, or cold, or miserable.

## THE RESISTANCE

There were some people in every country who co-operated with the Nazis, for example Quisling who took over as Prime Minister in Norway. These people were called collaborators and were generally hated by the rest of the population. The great majority of people just tried to get on with life as best they

| 6th December 1944 | 19th December 1944 | 9th January 1945 |
|---|---|---|
| It is reported that, as a result of Allied bombing, 20 million German people are now homeless. | The Germans stage a counter attack in the Ardennes, along the German border. The Allies are caught at their weakest point on a day of fog and cloud which stops the Allies using their air power. | The German counter attack in the Ardennes, called the "Battle of the Bulge", is over with an Allied win. |

could but in every country a *Resistance* movement began. In some countries the Resistance movement was very small and was outnumbered by the collaborators. In other countries, like Belgium, there were far more people in the Resistance movement than in collaboration with the Nazis.

## HELP FOR THE RESISTANCE

It was important for the Resistance to have contact with people fighting the war outside the occupied countries. Britain had a *Special Operations Executive* (SOE) responsible for contacting and helping Resistance movements. SOE would parachute men and women into occupied countries to help train Resistance fighters. They would also parachute equipment such as radios, explosives and guns to the Resistance. When equipped and trained there were many jobs for the Resistance fighters to do.

## GATHERING INFORMATION

In wartime knowing what your enemy is doing, or about to do, is a large part of the battle. The *Careless Talk Costs Lives* posters (see News and Information Section) show how important the British

Government knew this was. The Resistance people would collect information to send back to Britain. Information about troop movements; supply bases; numbers of tanks, guns and planes was always important and especially so when the plans for the Allied invasion of Europe were being made.

In Poland, where resistance was strong and the Germans were hated, the Polish Resistance (the Armia Krajowa) managed to get information about the V2 rocket to the Allies, even before the first rocket attacked Britain. The

Germans had been testing the V2s in Poland and one landed in a swamp near Warsaw. The Resistance found the rocket, hid it and then took it to pieces. They later sent information and parts of the rocket to Britain.

## CODES

Poland also sent the Allies the *Enigma Machine.* This was a German machine, rather like an early computer, which put important messages into code. The Germans never knew that the Allies had two of these machines and so never suspected that their codes had ever been broken.

DAILY MIRROR

WEATHER SHOWERS, COOLER (Details on Page 8)

Member of The Associated Press

Vol. 16. No. 282 C

New York, Friday, May 17, 1940

3 Cents Outside City Limits

FINAL EDITION ★★★

# NAZIS CUT DEEP INTO FRANCE

| 30th January 1945 | 14th February 1945 | 23rd February 1945 |
|---|---|---|
| Food riots have broken out in Berlin. In the bombed out city, civilians are cold and hungry and in fear have begun to dig trenches for shelter and defence in the inevitable Allied attack. | In the largest air raid ever, the RAF by night and the US airforce by day have almost totally destroyed the historic and beautiful city of Dresden. Sir Arthur "Bomber" Harris who planned the raid and believes in "terror bombing" has been much criticized for this raid. | After fierce fighting and great loss of life, the Americans have captured the island of Iwo Jima, 750 miles south of Tokyo. It will provide a base for the US airforce bombers to attack the Japanese mainland. |

Most of the information sent by the Resistance had to be put into code and then radioed, usually using morse code. This was to prevent the message falling into the hands of the Germans, although it also helped protect the radio operators who risked imprisonment or death for possessing an illegal radio.

## ESCAPE ROUTES

Another job the Resistance groups did was to organize the escape of people wanted by the Nazis. Very often these were escaped prisoners-of-war or Allied airmen who had parachuted from their aircraft over occupied country. If they were lucky enough to contact the Resistance, they would be passed from house to house, hiding in attics, cupboards and cellars until they reached either a neutral country or the coast – and a safe boat home.

## SABOTAGE

Attacks would be organized on troops and on convoys of supplies travelling by road and rail. The Resistance were also involved in blowing up bridges and generally making life difficult for the occupying army.

Sometimes factory workers would sabotage the work they were producing for the Germans by methods such as failing to put the explosives in a mine or grenade, or leaving a small but vital part out of a gun. Without the help of the various Resistance movements the Allies would have taken much longer to defeat the Axis Powers.

Hitler believed that if you ruled with fear and terror you could control everyone. The ordinary people of the Resistance who risked their lives to free their country proved him wrong.

# V SIGNS

## THE V. CAMPAIGN

In 1941 on the BBC's Belgian programme the idea of "V" as a symbol of Resistance was first used. "V" stood for "Victoire" in French and "Vriejheid" (Freedom) in Flemish, the two languages spoken in Belgium.

Very soon, throughout occupied Europe the "V" symbol was being chalked on walls, pavements and even German trucks and HQs. The "V" sign could be tapped out in Morse code, . . . - , and as the beginning of Beethoven's Fifth Symphony begins with three short notes, followed by one long one it became the opening music for BBC broadcasts into occupied Europe. The tune could also be whistled or hummed on the streets of Europe under the very noses of the occupying forces as a sign of resistance and defiance.

| 10th March 1945 | 25th March 1945 | 12th April 1945 |
|---|---|---|
| The centre of Tokyo is bombed by the US airforce. Thousands of incendiary (fire) bombs have caused much damage. | After discovering a railway bridge across the River Rhine at Remagen which the Germans have failed to destroy, the Allies cross the Rhine and Germany's last line of defence is gone. | President Roosevelt of the U.S.A. dies suddenly, just when victory for the Allies seems close. Germany is almost defeated and the war against Japan is going the Allies' way. Vice President Truman takes over as President. |

# THINGS TO DO

**1** The Resistance movements in each country were known by special names, usually in the language of that country. On the right is a list of names of European Resistance movements; by unscrambling the words on the far right you can find out to which country they belonged.

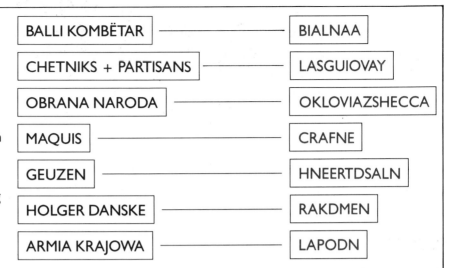

| | |
|---|---|
| BALLI KOMBËTAR | BIALNAA |
| CHETNIKS + PARTISANS | LASGUIOVAY |
| OBRANA NARODA | OKLOVIAZSHECCA |
| MAQUIS | CRAFNE |
| GEUZEN | HNEERTDSALN |
| HOLGER DANSKE | RAKDMEN |
| ARMIA KRAJOWA | LAPODN |

---

**2** *Simple letter shift code*
You can create your own code simply by substituting one letter for a letter, say three places away in the alphabet. If you do this for every letter you can write letters and messages to someone else if you tell them the secret of the code.
*Code maker & breaker:* Write out the alphabet on 2 pieces of paper.

ORIGINAL

| a b c d e f g h i j k l m n o p q r s t u v w x y z a |
|---|

| x y z | a b c d e f g h i j | k l m n o p | q r s t u v w x |

▲        ▲

CODE

In this code: e=h + p=s. So efp ald fp ilpq means ``his dog is lost.''
Now Solve: klt jxhb vlro ltk zlab

---

**3** *Symbol code*
Instead of using another letter to replace one letter in your code you can create 26 new symbols — one for each letter of the alphabet. Or you may want to write your own secret diary to be read only by you.

Example of a symbol code:

| a | b | c | d | e | f | g | h | i | j | k | l | m | n | o | p | q | r | s | t | u | v | w | x | y | z |
|---|---|---|---|---|---|---|---|---|---|---|---|---|---|---|---|---|---|---|---|---|---|---|---|---|---|

*Solve:*

---

| 25th April 1945 | 28th April 1945 | 29th April 1945 |
|---|---|---|
| Russian troops pushing back the Germans from the east and U.S. troops from the west meet and shake hands in Torgau, just south of Berlin. | Mussolini, Italy's former leader and friend of Hitler, is executed after his capture and trial by members of the Italian Resistance. | German troops fighting in Italy have surrendered to the Allies. |

# D-DAY

Soon after the retreat from Dunkirk in 1940, Churchill had realized that the only way to defeat Hitler was for the Allies to attack Europe which was then under his control. At first the Allies were not strong enough to do this and then later, they were involved with fighting in other areas of the world, particularly North Africa and the Far East. This meant that it was not until May 1943 that plans could be made to invade Europe and fight the Germans there. When the Italians surrendered in September 1943 the Germans were left alone in defending Europe. The invasion was a very bold scheme and secrecy was essential. It was codenamed *Operation Overlord* and was to take place on 'D'day.

## THE PLAN

The American General Eisenhower was in overall charge of Operation Overlord but had many other highly experienced officers working with him, such as the British General "Monty" Montgomery. They devised a plan to land men on the beaches of Normandy in Northern France. All the men and equipment would have to be transported by sea. The timing of the tides in the English Channel was of extreme importance. In order to deal with the thousands of mines and other defences the Germans had placed on the beaches, the landing would have to take place just after a low tide in the early morning. This would give the ships the cover of darkness to cross the channel. In June of 1944 the most suitable dates were 5th, 6th and 7th of the month. As June 5th was very stormy Tuesday 6th June 1944 became D-Day.

In order to take the Germans by surprise it was important they did not guess where or when D-Day would be. All sorts of tricks were used to make the Germans think the landings could take place elsewhere.

• Coded messages sent to the Resistance in Southern France in the hope that the Germans would pick them up, suggested that the landings may take place there.

• A whole dummy army camp built of cardboard near Dover gave the impression that the Landings would be at Calais.

The Germans were left

ROBERT HUNT LIBRARY

| 30th April 1945 | 7th May 1945 | 23rd May 1945 |
|---|---|---|
| Hitler is dead. He shot himself at his underground H.Q. in Berlin. The city is filled with Russian soldiers and more and more evidence of Hitler's Nazi death camps is being uncovered. | Victory in Euorpe. Germany signs an unconditional surrender to the Allies and celebrations throughout Britain and Europe begin. | The coalition government that has ruled Britain throughout the war resigns. There is to be a general election on July 5th. |

guessing as to where the real invasion would begin and had to spread out their soldiers and equipment along the entire French coast.

## THE MEN AND EQUIPMENT INVOLVED

- 50,000 men in the first attack
- 2 million soldiers in France in the following weeks
- 100,000 Resistance fighters to help

Equipment needed:

- 359 warships
- Over 1,000 minesweepers and auxiliary ships
- 4,000 landing craft
- 805 merchant ships
- 300 small boats
- 11,000 aircraft including fighters, bombers, transporters and gliders.

## PREPARATION

All the preparation and training took place in Britain. Two million soldiers practised on the beaches of Southern England, which were closed to civilians.

The roads were full of troops and equipment moving south. Sea ports and air bases were busy unloading American troops and supplies.

### PASSIERSCHEIN

An die britischen und amerikanischen Vorposten: Der deutsche Soldat, der diesen Passierschein vorzeigt, benutzt ihn als Zeichen seines ehrlichen Willens, sich zu ergeben. Er ist zu entwaffnen. Er muß gut behandelt werden. Er hat Anspruch auf Verpflegung und, wenn nötig, ärztliche Behandlung. Er wird so bald wie möglich aus der Gefahrenzone entfernt.

### SAFE CONDUCT

The German soldier who carries this safe-conduct is using it as a sign of his genuine wish to give himself up. He is to be disarmed, to be well looked after, to receive food and medical attention as required, and is to be removed from the danger zone as soon as possible.

In factories and ship yards throughout Britain, ships of all sorts were taking shape. Tanks had to be adapted for the beaches and the mines and obstacles they would meet there. A major project in the shipyards was the construction in sections of artificial harbours

called *Mulberries.* Each huge section had to be towed across the channel and tied in position just off the Normandy coast. Linked together the sections formed a harbour for ships to unload men and supplies close to the coast.

Production of all the other weapons and equipment needed by the army, navy and airforce had to be increased so everyone in the country was working as hard as they could.

Despite all this activity the precise date and location for D-Day never leaked out. Indeed, people in Britain were taken by surprise when the news came that the invasion had begun.

### THE INVASION

Although the Germans too were taken by surprise they still had a large number of tanks and men to defend the beaches. After dropping paratroopers, the RAF and U.S. Airforce provided cover from the air. They dropped bombs and machine gunned the concrete bunkers from which German soldiers defended the beaches. The Navy guns on ships offshore bombarded the coast. In amongst all this bombing, firing and fighting the Allied soldiers had to leave their landing craft, bringing with them equipment such as tanks,

| 31st May 1945 | 6th June 1945 | 21st June 1945 |
|---|---|---|
| By now a large number of Nazi leaders and Gestapo have been rounded up and imprisoned while the Allies decide what to do with them. They are expected to stand trial for the terrible crimes they have committed. | It has been announced in Moscow that Russia will take control of nearly half of Germany. This will mean that the Americans and British will have to withdraw from some of the German territory they have responsibility for at the moment. | The Americans have finally captured the island of Okinawa, 300 miles south of Tokyo. The battle began on 1st April 1945 and has cost many American and Japanese lives. |

and large guns. The first soldiers had to deal with the beach defences of obstacles and mines. Once they had cleared the way, more soldiers followed.

By the end of the first day 156,000 American, British and Canadian troops had crossed the Channel to France and had taken or "liberated" up to ten miles inland. In some areas they had fought fiercely to move forward only a little; in other less well-defended areas the soldiers made rapid progress.

### ONWARD FROM D-DAY

From the landings in Normandy the Allies still had much work to do. The ships continued to ferry men and supplies across the Channel. The U.S. Airforce and RAF bombed German supply routes, railways and bridges.

From D-Day there was nearly another year of fierce fighting in Europe, as the Allies gradually liberated the occupied countries and before Germany surrendered in May 1945.

# D-DAY AND THE RESISTANCE

When D-Day, the invasion of Europe by the Allies, came, the French Resistance were of vital importance. Their job was to blow up bridges, railways and power stations to stop fresh German troops reaching Normandy. They cut telephone wires to make German communications difficult. Road blocks, barricades and blacked out road signs set up by the Resistance added to the Germans' problems.

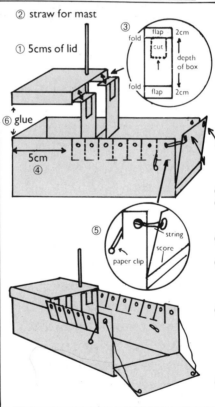

② straw for mast
① 5cms of lid
③ fold / flap / 2cm / cut / depth of box / fold / flap / 2cm
⑥ glue
5cm
④
⑤ string / score / paper clip

# THINGS TO DO

**1** On your Operations Map of Europe mark the Normandy Beaches. Make some flags for the Allies; Britain, Russia and U.S.A. You can follow the chronology at the bottom of each page and replace the German flag with an Allied flag as each country is liberated.

**2** *Make your own landing craft*

You will need: shoe box with lid; string; garden twine or dark coloured wool; sellotape; glue; pencil; pair of scissors with pointed end; two brass opening paper clips; lump of plasticine; wax crayons.

### LANDING CRAFT

① Cut 5cms off lid
② With scissors and a lump of plasticine behind make a hole for the straw radio mast
③ Cut out 2 of the shapes circled, from the rest of the lid
④ Cut slots down both sides of the box, apart from 5cms indicated. Make a hole in each flap for guns. Don't forget the plasticine behind!
⑤ Make a score line carefully (with scissors or sharp pencil) and cut down at corners to line. Make holes as before. With wool or string thread through holes and wrap end around paper clip, inserted as shown.
⑥ Glue lid and shapes from ③ sticking flaps to lid and the box.

| 26th June 1945 | 15th July 1945 | 16th July 1945 |
|---|---|---|
| Delegates from fifty countries sign a Charter to bring into being the United Nations. | The blackout and dim out are finally over in Britain. Many people gather in the streets to view the lights from shops, street lamps and neon signs. | While the first atomic bomb tests are being carried out in America, a fleet of Royal Navy and US Navy warships shell Tokyo from their offshore positions. |

Against that he had to think about the American soldiers who would die in an invasion of Japan. President Truman also had to consider the evidence that the Japanese had been ill-treating and starving Allied prisoners-of-war. The suffering of these prisoners would be shortened by ending the war as soon as possible and the dropping of an atomic bomb could do just that.

## HIROSHIMA AND NAGASAKI

President Truman delivered a warning to the Japanese. "If Japan does not surrender, atomic bombs will be dropped on her war industries." No surrender came and on 6th August 1945 the first atomic bomb was dropped on Hiroshima. Three days later a second atomic bomb was dropped on Nagasaki. Japan surrendered and the 15th August 1945 became known as V.J. (Victory in Japan) Day. This marked the end of the Second World War and was the cause of great celebrations.

Meanwhile in Japan people were continuing to die from the injuries caused by the explosion, fireball and radiation from the two atomic bombs. Over seventy thousand people had died immediately and in Hiroshima and Nagasaki hardly a building was left standing.

Forty-five years later, people in Hiroshima and Nagasaki are still dying from the effects of the atomic bombs. What was not fully understood in 1945 was that the radiation from the bomb was long-lived and could cause cancers of the blood, bone and tissue that would continue to kill the people of Hiroshima and Nagasaki for many years to come.

### THINGS TO DO

**1** Do you think the Allies were right to drop the atomic bombs on Hiroshima and Nagasaki? What arguments can you put forward to support your opinion?

**2** Many poems were written about the war. Try to write a poem of your own about war. You might like to concentrate on one thing that happened in the war or write a poem about war in general.

**3** Keep your own war file. From present day newspapers and magazines keep cuttings of stories and pictures about the war. Make notes about any television or radio programmes or books you read that deal with the Second World War.

| KILLED IN THE WAR – Asia and Pacific | Armed Forces | Civilians | | Armed Forces | Civilians |
|---|---|---|---|---|---|
| American | 50,000 | – | Chinese | 3,500,000 | 10,000,000 |
| New Zealand | 10,000 | – | Japanese | 1,700,000 | 360,000 |
| Australian | 30,000 | – | Total all nations | 5,330,000 | 10,360,000 |
| British | 40,000 | – | | | |
| | | | Total worldwide losses | 53,300,000 | |

# ANSWERS

## The Beginning of the War

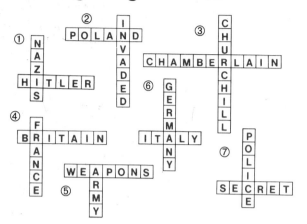

① N A Z I S
② P O L A N D
H I T L E R
③ C H U R C H I L L
C H A M B E R L A I N
I N V A D E D
⑥ G E R M A N Y
④ B R I T A I N — F R A N C E
I T A L Y
⑦ P O L I C E
W E A P O N S
⑤ A R M Y
S E C R E T

## Shelters

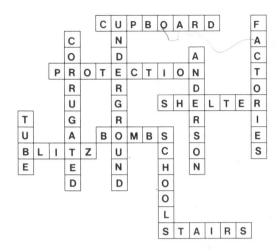

C U P B O A R D
C O R R U G A T E D
P R O T E C T I O N
S H E L T E R
T U B E
B L I T Z
B O M B S
F A C T O R I E S
U N D E R G R O U N D
S C H O O L
S T A I R S

## School

E D U C A T I O N
R A — R U L E
W A R
A R T
I N C H
E V A C U A T E
R A F — A D U L T S
P E N C I L — R E A D

## The Blackout

(word search with circled answers: INCONVENIENT, RIBBONS, BOX, AIR RAID, REGULATIONS, CURTAINS, DIM OUT, GAS MASK, ANTI AIRCRAFT, PROTECTION, GRASS, LUMINOUS)

## Work

(word search with circled answers: POLICEMAN, GOOGLE, DOCKER, BUS DRIVER, KEEPER, MERCHANT SEAMAN, COAL MINER, TRAIN DRIVER)

## Resistance

| | | |
|---|---|---|
| BALLI KOMBËTAR | —— | ALBANIA |
| CHETNIKS + PARTISANS | —— | YUGOSLAVIA |
| OBRANA NARODA | —— | CZECHOSLOVAKIA |
| MAQUIS | —— | FRANCE |
| GEUZEN | —— | NETHERLANDS |
| HOLGER DANSKE | —— | DENMARK |
| ARMIA KRAJOWA | —— | POLAND |

klt jxhb vlro ltk zlab

꒱ꬷꬣ/ꬵ°ꬼꭅ/°#ꬰ/ꬵꬵ꒑ꬴ·ꬴ/ꬾꬻꬰꬷꬽꬴꬵ꒒

NOW MAKE YOUR OWN CODE    MAKE YOUR OWN SYMBOL ALPHABET

## Progress of the War

H U N G A R Y
B E L G I U M
F R A N C E
L U X E M B O U R G
J A P A N
D E N M A R K
I T A L Y

G I B R A L T A R
A U S T R A L I A
I N D I A
W E S T I N D I E S
U S A
R U S S I A
C A N A D A

FIFE EDUCATION COMMITTEE

KING'S ROAD P. SCHOOL

## Acknowledgements

The publishers are grateful to the following:

The Imperial War Museum, the Museum of London and the Robert Hunt Library for permission to reproduce photographs. Brooke Bond Oxo and Cadbury's Bournville for permission to reproduce advertisements. *Good Housekeeping* for permission to use articles and other material from *The Best of Good Housekeeping*.

Acknowledgement is also due to Wilfred Acornley; Dudley Andrew; William and Audrey Brownlie; Ian Butterworth; Alfred Dickman; Muriel Good; Laura and Richard Hall; Elsie Jacobs; Olive Linford; Major Cyril Peckitt; Alan Robertson at Leisure Solutions; Jenny Salter; and Margaret Sterling for providing many of the objects pictured in this book.